9.99

Awesome God

Sara Maitland was born in 1950. In 1979 her first novel, *Daughter of Jerusalem*, won the Somerset Maugham Award. Since then she has published novels, short stories and non-fiction, including works of theology like *A Map of the New Country*, *A Big Enough God* and *Angel and Me*. She has broadcast and lectured extensively, teaches creative writing and also writes on mental health issues. In 2000, the younger of her children having left home, she moved to the top of a Durham moor, where she is researching for a cultural history of silence, and also trying to work out how to live a contemporary version of a silent life.

For Chris Long, Emily Aaron, Adam Lee,
Catherine Briggs, Adam McHenry, and especially
Iain Bell (who enjoyed the 'issues'),
with love and thanks.

Awesome God
Creation, Commitment and Joy

Sara Maitland

SPCK

First published in Great Britain in 2002 by
Society for Promoting Christian Knowledge
Holy Trinity Church
Marylebone Road
London NW1 4DU

British Library Cataloguing-in-Publication Data
A catalogue record for this book is available from the British Library

ISBN 0-281-05419-3

Typeset by FiSH Books, London WC1
Printed in Great Britain by
The Cromwell Press, Trowbridge, Wiltshire

Contents

Note: Here and there throughout the text you will find some 'parables'. Like the biblical ones, these are just stories. It is up to each reader to decide which ones, if any, have 'significance'; and what that significance might be.

Introduction

At the moment there are a great many books being published, and we must therefore assume being bought and read, about the relationship, if any, between science and God. Often there is something adversarial about these books (and articles and television and radio programmes). It sometimes feels as though God and science are engaged in a mortal fight for the ownership of our minds and hearts. God and science are frequently treated as though one of them were a slightly pathetic fairy tale princess, locked up in a tower by the other one, who is of course a wicked witch. At the ground level, some atheists and some 'believers', both claiming to be heroic knights, well armed and glowing with virtue, fight it out to the death to rescue the princess. Whether or not she wants or needs rescuing is never asked.

If you are theologically inclined, the fashionable thing to do at the moment is to write a book on this theme. You look at the contemporary sciences and see if you can prove that God is there.

Well, you can't.

The best you can do – and it has been very ably done[1] – is to prove that you can't prove that God is *not* there.

On the one hand, as C. S. Lewis pointed out, 'absence of proof is not proof of absence'. On the other, it is well nigh impossible to prove a negative.

The people who *want* to find God tend to be satisfied with this possibility: they are theists or deists. The people who want not to find God tend to accept that the absence of evidence demonstrates an absence of God: they are atheists. (Both these groups, if their beliefs about God are based solely on the evidence from science, are bad scientists. They have come to a fixed conclusion without sufficient proof.)

Some people, clearer about the logic, tend to accept that the question is not provable either way: they are agnostics.

Incidentally, the largest group of people today, regardless of what they think about science, decide that they are not really that interested in God: in other words, they are adiaphorists (a useful and descriptive term that deserves wider recognition).

The only strange thing about all this is that anyone should be surprised or upset by the failure to prove the existence, or otherwise, of God. Philosophy, which deals in abstracts, ideas, infinities, eternities, and ethics, failed to produce a proof of God in over two thousand years of hard work. It seems unlikely that the hard sciences, which deal with actual solid things like matter, are going to do much better in less than half the time.

Moreover, most contemporary atheists (especially the converting kind) are not very clear about what kind of God they are trying to prove cannot (scientifically) exist. Gods come in a wide variety of flavours, so to speak, many of which are completely contradictory.

Just as a round-up, and by no means a complete one, some of the styles of God that have attracted belief from human beings include:

The subtle variations of monotheism (only one God); polytheism (lots of Gods, arranged in a wide variety of social hierarchies); pantheism (everything is God); animism (everything is infused by the spirit of God); tribalism (a god, or gods, who belongs exclusively to us, and may even be our human ancestors – your gods may well exist, they are simply not relevant); more complex disembodied notions which may even eschew the word God – like Buddhism; and many others.

Within these groups there is also a considerable range of lifestyle options.

There are mean gods – violent, aggressive, highly punitive gods, who are none the less amenable to bribery, often of a very crude sort.

There are gods who are very like people: superheroes really – although stronger and more mobile, they essentially act like we do, having preferences and prejudices, conflicting with one another and engaging in 'human' activities, such as falling in love, getting jealous, having sex – both with one another or with humans.

There are gods who are not omnipotent (all powerful). There are even tragic gods who are probably not going to win in the end. The strange beauty of Norse mythology lies precisely here – Balder, the beautiful, the best of the gods, is dead. Although his divine comrades will march out boldly to Ragnarok, to the last battle, at best the issue is in the balance, the forces of dark and chaos may very well be victorious.

Some gods are negligent; they have business other than involving themselves with humanity, or even with the world. Some are more simply 'absent'. (It would be impossible to prove the existence or non-existence of an absent god. A god who caused the Big Bang and then withdrew totally from the consequences would be perfectly plausible, though also perfectly boring.)

An unusual but distinct deity, whom I offer just to underline the point, is an Inuit god – one who is well-meaning but totally incompetent. The entire ritual task of the priests of this cult is to sing lullabies to keep the god asleep (since awake he will try to help and the results will be disastrous). The most important moral precept is not to fight – since the noise of this will wake the god up.

There are dynamic gods who move and act and change; and there are static gods. One major version of the Christian God is like this – the Unmoved Mover, 'the platform for the lever'. (It is rather unclear where Christianity got this idea from – certainly not from our Hebrew roots.)

Obviously it makes a difference what sort of God you are looking for when it comes to deciding how you will 'prove' it. When you meet someone in a pub who says she or he is the Second Coming of the Son of God, the reason you do not believe them is at least in part because that person is not behaving in the way you believe the Second Coming of the Son of God would behave. This means you have some ideas about how such an incarnation should behave. If you believed in a highly violent God and the person in the pub is not hitting anyone, that might constitute negative proof.

But usually nowadays when we are told by members of the Western scientific community that we 'cannot believe in God', they mean the Christian God or some version thereof. We cannot believe in this God because we cannot 'prove' it. This is interesting because in that respect such people believe exactly what Christianity has always taught.

Christianity has always known that you cannot prove the existence of God by any 'logical' method. This does not mean of course that you cannot think about God, speculate about God, say intelligent things about God, question the value of God, or even worship God. It just means that you cannot prove the existence of God. Indeed, many of the great Christian thinkers have gone further: they have argued that it is part of the essential nature of God, the love and immensity and power of the divine, that you cannot prove the existence of God. If God is 'love' as Christianity has taught, then obviously you can't 'prove' God's existence. Even human love is not 'provable' (though it certainly exists). It has to be taken on trust.

Christianity, like Judaism and Islam, are what are called 'revealed' religions. We know about God only what God reveals to us; we know about God only because God, who is unknowable and unprovable by human methods, generously lets us know.

So although we cannot know the nature of God and cannot prove the existence of God, we can know quite a lot about God, because God chooses to reveal quite a lot.

God has revealed, and continues to reveal, God, quite simply, as a gift.

I say 'quite simply', but of course it is not simple at all. God appears to enjoy crossword puzzles. God's self-revelation is, as it were, in code: a set of cryptic clues. Of course, this may be because God is cleverer than we are; can use more languages, more kinds of communications, more complex sets of signs, than we can even dream of. God may be (and I believe is) up to something larger, more complex, and more refined than we seem able to imagine. It may also be because of material limitations. Just as the physical structure of how it is to be a human being will prevent anyone ever running a three-second mile, so the physical-neural structure of how it is to be a human being may actually make it impossible for us to speak a language or generate a thought that embraces eternity. We exist in time. We need time and place to be human, but that in itself may make it impossible for us to see God clearly, for us to perceive or comprehend eternity – which is not 'more-time' but 'not-time'.

Just look at how impossibly difficult most of us have found it to take in what astro-physicists are saying: there was no time 'before' the Big Bang. You cannot talk about 'before the Big Bang' any more than you can talk about 'north of the North Pole'. I believe that, but I can't quite get it inside my head, into my imagination. My mind – which can cope with angels, miracles, and the virgin birth – simply cannot cope with there being 'no before-time'. I find it impossible to think in those terms; and I suspect other people have this problem too. We are not well designed to think outside of time.

If God cannot be proved through logic or science, how do we get to know about God? How does God do the revealing thing?

Different religions, even those who share the idea about God's self-revealing, have different answers to this question.

Judaism, the oldest of these, believes that God's revelation comes through his dealings with a particular people, as recorded in a book (commonly called the Pentateuch – the first five books of the Hebrew Scriptures). Jews also believe in a Law that was given to them through Moses in an unmediated visionary experience; in a Covenant – a contract between the Jewish people and God; and that God reveals the divine nature in the history of the people.

Islam believes that the One God – Allah, who is 'unprovable' – revealed himself directly to his prophet Mohammed, in a similar, but more extended vision, and dictated a revelation that Mohammed took down and recorded in full in the book that is now known as the Koran. Some of this book has a great deal in common with the Hebrew book, and some of it does not. The Koran is regarded as a complete revelation – although it may require interpretation, the study of it cannot add to it.

Judaism believes also in a book. Christians believe that God's generous revelation is given through the Jewish Book *and* the Jewish Covenant, *and* through the life, death, and resurrection of Jesus Christ, which is recorded in an additional book. These two books together are called 'the Scriptures' (which means 'the writings'). Christians further believe that God is revealed through the history of interpreting and meditating and thinking about those Scriptures within the Christian community. This is known as 'the Tradition'. (Like the Scriptures, this can be trusted because of the Holy Spirit, who is a continuing source of revelation.) Some, but not all, Christians also believe that God chooses to be fully present, to 'reveal the divine', in certain acts of worship called 'sacraments'.

However, these three religions, and many others, although they have different languages to describe it, share the belief that God can be known in the 'mighty works'. That is to say in the creation, understood very widely. Not just a one-off starting gun, but in history, in personalities, and in 'the way things are'. The way the world is, the way it is to be a human being, the way history goes, the way nature behaves; in the laws of the universe and the realities of our humanity.

I believe in God. I am a Christian. For a whole range of reasons, some of which will emerge in the course of this book, I believe that the Scriptures, the Tradition, and the creation are sources of God's greatest gift to us – the desire and the ability to know something about God. I believe that the created order is God's 'mighty work' – that everything we know, whether it comes from 'inside us' or 'outside us', is part of an extraordinary and powerful act: the making, the creating, the sustaining of the universe.

Also, quite separately, I believe that you can learn something about makers of things by the thing that they make. For example, you can learn something about authors by reading their books: provided, of course, that you read properly, carefully, respectfully, attentively and without too many preconceptions (or at least with some awareness of what your preconceptions are).

In this book I am going to try to look at the creation, using all the information that contemporary science provides us with – or, rather, all of it that I am capable of understanding – in the assumption (the preconception) that it was made by God. I am not looking for evidence for God, but evidence of God – in much the same way that art critics use the very shape and weight of brushstrokes as evidence as to which artist painted a particular picture. God made the world, so it must be marked with God's brushstrokes; God's voice patterns; God's fingerprints; God's DNA. What sort of picture of God can I build up from this evidence?

Or, to put it another way, I want to bring to the study of some of the discoveries of contemporary scientists the same sort of approach that many Christian spiritual and mystical writers suggest that we bring to the study of the Scriptures. God is *here*, we say, from a position of faith. What does this particular *here* have to tell us about God and ourselves?

I am starting then from two assumptions. One: God made the universe. Two: there is a connection, an intimate and sometimes painful connection, between what a person *is* and what they do or make. I want to look attentively at what we know of the creation and ask questions like, 'What sort of God might have made this sort of world? What can we say about a God who does this sort of thing? How do we stand in relation to a God like this?'

The psalmist wrote:

> Understand, O dullest of people!
> Fools, when will you be wise?
> He who planted the ear, does he not hear?
> He who formed the eye, does he not see?
> He who chastens the nations does he not chastise?
> He who teaches us knowledge knows our thoughts.[2]

This psalm writer was not engaged in any 'argument by design' exercise. He was not saying, as many nineteenth-century theologians said, that the universe was so well ordered, so fitted for human life and so complex, that there had to be a God to explain it all. This poet, a better word here than theologian, is not endeavouring to prove that God exists as a logical or deductive consequence of eyes and ears existing. The existence of God is a poetic (and theological) certainty to the writer. What he is exploring is what we can learn or say about a God whom we believe *did* create eyes and ears.

This psalm crystallizes the approach I am hoping to take, but nowadays the questions feel a bit trickier. The God who made – for example – reverse time in atomic particles, random mutation in therapsids, black holes in the far-flung galaxies, errors in the memory, who allows infinities to come in an infinite range of sizes, and oysters to be able to tell the phases of the moon – does this God not . . . not *what*?

Or, as Paul puts it: '. . . for the invisible things of Him from the creation of the world are clearly seen, being

The earth feels solid beneath my feet. It is the staple measure of solidity. But it is not solid; not stable; barely safe. Vast slabs of rock, the continents, float on a sea, a deeper ocean of liquid rock. These slabs, the tectonic plates, drift on a current, slowly inexorably moving, shifting. There are heavy plates which make up the land masses, and lighter plates which form the ocean floors.

Bump. They bump into each other, the heavy plates riding up over the lighter ones and pushing the lighter ones down. Down into the melted matter, where they disintegrate. Oceans disappear. Once the Sinai desert was all sea – there are fossilized mollusc-shell casts to be found by the handful. The huge desert cliffs of terror and beauty were shaped under water.

Sometimes the heavy plates come up against other heavy plates: the irresistible force and the immovable object. They collide, jostle, uneasy, always moving. Where they make contact they push up mountain ranges, folds and fragments of their edges. They bulge downwards too – shoving the roots of mountains into the oceans of soft rock. Like trees, when the roots die the mountains collapse. Once northern Scotland was part of a mountain range as high as the Himalayas. When they meet, they shove, push, bump, grind, like children in a playground. As they move towards or along each other, they groan, jerk, twitch, slip, skid. There is a seam where they come together. The fiery liquid of the hot ocean can push through: volcanoes, earthquakes, tremors, geysers. 'Faults', we call these places dismissively: like calling a tiger a cat.

They shift, shove, moan, creak. Africa inches northwards, greedily gobbling up the Mediterranean. America drifts towards Europe; the Atlantic narrows and Pacific widens. The mountains moan in pain and fear. Gas and lava muscle their way to the surface, seeking release from intolerable pressure: heat pressure, weight pressure, pressure. There are special points of danger. There are no points of safety.

They are moving all the time, these dense, heavy, immeasurably shifting and dishonest plates of the earth's surface. They move at about the same speed as your finger nails grow.

understood by the things that are made, even his eternal power and godhead.'

It is this connection that I want to try and explore.

The word 'science' derives from a Latin verb *scio*: 'to know'. The sciences are the things we know. I shall be using the word quite widely. I am not planning to look just at the 'hard' sciences – physics, biology, and chemistry – but at the strange science (if it is a science) of mathematics and the 'soft' sciences like sociology, psychology, and linguistics.

There are five immediate problems with this proposal (there are probably some more, but I don't know what they are yet). Two are to do with me:

1 I am neither a scientist nor a theologian. I do not have the 'proper qualifications'. I am a Christian, a writer of fiction (a liar in Plato's definition). When it comes to the subjects of this book, I am an amateur. But I do not apologize for that, because the word 'amateur' means 'lover' (one who loves – from the Latin word *amo*) and nobody learns about something so carefully and tenderly as a lover does.
2 I am part of the creation (so are you; so is everybody; so is everything). The scientific method says you are meant to study things 'objectively', from the outside inwards; not to get over-involved or emotional about one's subject. But there is simply nowhere that I, or any of us, can position ourselves to look at the creation from 'outside'. There is no outside. I cannot be audience because I am part of the show. I cannot be objective because I am part of the subject of the investigation.

The other problems are not to do with me, or not directly:

3 The Christian faith has always had an enormous difficulty in working out how to deal with new forms of knowledge. This is a bit odd really: you might

reasonably think that a religion that claimed to believe in an all-knowing, all-powerful God, an enormous infinite, eternal God who none the less was committed to revealing that divinity to human beings, would be deeply gratified when scientists turned up and said, 'Look, we've discovered this new thing.' You might think that such a religion would look a bit smug and say, 'We told you so. What can you find next?' or, better still, would say, 'Thank you.' But no. Absolutely not. Christianity has tended not even to say, 'We think you're wrong, because . . .', but instead to take a firm line and say, as it said to Galileo, 'Shut up or we'll kill you.' This particularly applies to scientific knowledge – in some other areas of culture, music and architecture particularly, Christianity has done very much better.[3]

This is not a twenty-first-century problem: right from the beginning when the early Church realized that the Second Coming was not as imminent as they had originally thought, there has been a running difficulty in processing and accepting basic factual information: the conquest of the Holy Lands by Islam; the desire for a vernacular Bible; the observations of Copernicus, Kepler, and Galileo; the discovery of the New World; fossils and evolution; archaeology and biblical scholarship; the equality of women – all these discoveries have generated unease and opposition from the Christian Church. This reluctance means that most of the time Christianity has a very creaky and out-of-date language, imagination, and culture. (The Roman Catholic Church eventually 'reinstated' Galileo at the very end of the twentieth century – that means that for over three hundred years they had to talk about God's creative power in the universe without being able to incorporate honestly and openly the most basic observations of astronomers.) Liturgical language and our imaginations probably won't catch up for another hundred years or so. This dragging deficiency has become so acute that many people feel the need to ask,

'Have the wells run dry?' Is the core imagery of Christian theology and poetry now incapable of speaking to us? I don't believe this actually, but all Christians have to take this question seriously: if they haven't run dry, then they are certainly extremely clogged up with old rubbish; the fresh and cooling streams are not exactly bubbling up in the desert.

4 Scientists want to insist on the 'objectivity' of the scientific method. I'm not complaining here about 'relativity' and Einstein's description of the way that the position of the observer affects the thing observed, but something much older and in a way simpler. Scientists cannot resist making poetry, making mythology. They are not at all scientific in this sense. For example, the Big Bang was not big (it was sub-atomic) and it was not a bang (it was necessarily silent, since in the absence of time and atmosphere there was nothing to convey sound waves and there was nothing to receive them either). But we like the Big Bang; it is the sort of creative moment we can relate to. Interestingly, the French existentialist writer, Albert Camus, in what is probably the best atheist propaganda essay ever written, *The Myth of Sisyphus*, complains about this mythologizing tendency of the scientists:

> Of whom and of what indeed can I say 'I know that!'. . . you describe [the world] to me and you teach me to classify it. You enumerate its laws and in my thirst for knowledge I admit that they are true. You take apart its mechanism and my hope increases. At the final stage you teach me that this wondrous and multi-coloured universe can be reduced to the atom and that the atom itself can be reduced to the electron. All this is good and I wait for you to continue. But you tell me of an invisible planetary system in which electrons gravitate around a nucleus. You explain the world to me with an image. I realise then that you have been reduced to

> poetry... That science which was to teach me everything ends up in a hypothesis, that lucidity founders in metaphor, that uncertainty is resolved in a work of art.[4]

I do not want to suggest that scientists are 'cheating'. I *do* want us to be aware that just as Christian theology has an enormous problem with language, so does the most sophisticated science.

This may be the very nature of language: words are not things – they are representations of things. They are themselves in a way poems; images of reality. Indeed, some people now believe they are independent of, and possibly even more 'real' than, the material objects that they represent. Perhaps, therefore, it is impossible to speak without being 'reduced to poetry'. The point here is that we must be very careful when scientists claim to be 'telling the truth'. The Big Bang, like most scientific descriptions, is a story too, though a story of a particular kind.

5 Contemporary Western society has a real problem with the nature of 'proof', which means different things in different contexts. Perhaps the real difficulty is with 'trust'. It is not that we don't 'trust' anyone, it is that we have the most eccentric (and unreasonable) ways of deciding who or what we do trust (for example, we are, culturally, more afraid of BSE than of alcohol – which is completely irrational). This problem can be seen in the way we don't seem able to distinguish between the meanings of 'I believe', 'I think', and 'I feel'.[5] So, we can't believe in God because someone else tells us that God exists. But we do (by and large) believe in quarks because someone tells us they exist. On the whole, it is more counter-intuitive to believe in quarks than in God, but this does not affect our belief systems. I believe the world is spherical and revolving both around its own axis and around the sun. But that is not what my senses experience: I *feel* it is flat and the sun moves across the

> sky from east to west. It is not even a question of going with the majority: globally and historically, far more human beings have believed in God than in quarks. This makes it very hard to argue, persuade, or even learn without cheating, or vulgarizing.
>
> Deference, obedience, and believing everything you are told are all very dangerous and I would not wish to encourage them. But unconsidered faith, illogical faith, and faith based solely on my own misperceptions of my own 'feelings' or experiences, without an understanding of how or why I give credit to these things, is just as dubious. Before I can ask, 'What do I believe?' I need to ask myself, 'What do I mean by belief?'

These problems are all real. They get in the way of what I am trying to do. But it is because of problems like these that thinking about God is fun. It is not like learning your times-tables, or taking a multiple-choice test: you have to stay on your toes, and keep your eyes peeled. The subject matter will not stay still and let you probe it, strip it down, pin it to a board and dissect it, subject it to the rules of logic and reason. Actually I suspect that this is part of what God chooses to reveal. Bertrand Russell said that he could not become a Christian because there was not a word in the Gospels in praise of intelligence. This is true, but as Russell ought to have known, God is revealed also in the creation and there is a great deal there that speaks in praise of an intelligent, complex, intricate, challenging God.

Let's be clear: the modern scientific method has delivered wondrous goods into our laps and our hearts,[6] but – as in all the best stories – there has been a bill to meet. Part of the price has been to reduce the idea of 'reason' to a sort of instrument for calculation, classification, and systematization; and then to declare that all other patterns of thought are irrational, unreasonable. But there is an older sense of the word 'reason': until Newtonian physics were well established, reason was seen as 'the candle of the Lord'.[7] Reason was not something outside, or over and above, the world, an instrument that could be applied to subjects in order to manage them. Far from distancing human beings from the creation, reason sprang up from it in the widest sense.

The existence of God cannot be proved, but that does not mean that it is not reasonable to believe in God. There are lots of good reasons for believing in God actually (as well as an almost equal number for not believing in God), ranging from the personal witness of a great number of individuals across a great swathe of history, through to the fact that religious faith makes so many neo-Darwinian scientists so cross.

Reason and proof are not the same thing. It suggests a narrowing of our cultural and linguistic grasp that we should want them to be. We need a bit more of the attitude of the seventeenth century, when Jeremy Taylor (no intellectual slouch by anyone's definition) could write of 'reason' in terms that make it sound more like poetry than what is nowadays called science:

> Reason is such a box of quicksilver that it abides nowhere: it dwells in no settled mansion: it is like a dove's neck, or a changeable taffeta; it looks to me otherwise than it looks to you, who do not stand in the same light as I do . . . it wanders up and down like a floating island, or like that which we call the life blood.[8]

It is this sort of reason, this imaginative creative force, that we have to keep in mind as we plunge into the intricate folds of the creation; of the world which is the only world we have got.

Theology and Science

1 'In the beginning God made heaven and earth.'
2 For causes that we cannot know, and actually cannot discuss – since what a cause and effect could possibly *be* without time is not thinkable – matter, time, and space came into being spontaneously and forcibly at a singularity.[1]

There have been a great many attempts recently to try and claim that these two statements are compatible; that they somehow say the 'same thing'. In other words, to try to merge them into one, to argue that the Genesis account is just a different way of expressing the Big Bang theory (or that the Big Bang is just a different way of expressing the Genesis account of the creation).

I don't think this is entirely honest. They do not say the same thing; and trying to force them to do so, or to pretend that they already do, adds to the confusion rather than clarifying anything.

They do not say the same, not because one of them is 'true' and the other 'false' (I personally think that both of them are true), but because the sources and the kinds of information they present are not the same and cannot be compared to each other in this way.

While there is a broad agreement about the sort of statement that no. 2 is (a lay person's, radically simplified account of a 'state of the science' description of the origin of the universe), there is far less agreement about what sort of statement no. 1 is. I am not sure that I know what sort of statement it is; but I am very sure about what sort of statement it is *not*.

It is not a 'wrong' or bad scientific statement. A great many people speak as though the value of the Bible is diminished by the fact that they cannot agree with its science. Nobody thinks that the pleasures of Monopoly are diminished because it gets the prices of London streets wrong. Monopoly is neither an estate agent's brochure nor an economics textbook. Nobody expects it to be. But while there is a great deal said about 'the pre-scientific world view' and the modern scientific mind, we seem to find it hard to accept fully that Genesis was written down in a pre-scientific era so that whatever it is, it is not likely to be a scientific text.

It is not an ethical instruction. No moral consequences flow from it. Somewhere between the people who want to treat the Bible as failed science and the people who want to treat it as a perfect etiquette book, we have lost sight of what it might actually be.

We can't even be sure what the people who wrote it down thought it was. We do know that substantial sections of Genesis got rewritten, edited, corrected, and sometimes interleaved, which is why, for example, there are two different versions of the creation of human beings.[2] This suggests to me that at various times even the community who held this book to be the true revelation of God from God, were not absolutely sure what sort of statement it was. This makes it hard to know precisely how they believed it.

We also know that the Hebrew people drew no pictures, eschewed visual representation, but had a strong musical and verbal culture. They expressed themselves poetically, apparently with fluency and ease and sincerity. Their theology was a poetic theology, not a scientific theology. It is worth trying to think about the Genesis creation story (or stories) as poetic theology rather than as science.

The medieval Christian culture apparently read the story differently from this, as well as differently from how we might read it today. They had a 'science' of sorts; they knew that the world was at the centre of the universe, and eight spheres revolved around it. (It is important to note that this is not the model proposed in Genesis.) But, on the whole, they saw the world *analogically*: everything in it was made *for* human beings, not primarily for their delight, but for their edification. This is why the medieval mind could happily call theology the 'Queen of Sciences': the ordering and interpreting force, which gave rhythm and harmony to the pursuit of knowledge. The world was made up of symbols and signs specifically and deliberately designed by God to remind and assist us in the search for our true homeland in heaven.

Thus the robin has a red breast to remind us of Christ's passion.

Rocks are hard to remind us of the toughness of Peter (and of the enduring power of the papacy).

Pelicans cut their own breasts to feed their young with their blood so that we shall be reminded (on the presumably infrequent occasions when we happen to encounter a nesting pelican) of Jesus' suffering and life-giving love for us all.

Most events in the Hebrew Scriptures were understood as 'types' or pre-notifications of events that were going to happen in the New Testament. 'We can hardly imagine a state of mind in which all material objects were regarded as symbols of spiritual truths or episodes in sacred history. Yet unless we make this effort of imagination, mediaeval art is largely incomprehensible.'[3]

It is equally hard for us to realize that until the Enlightenment people had very little difficulty believing several things at once – even if they were contradictory. Very early in the Church's history, Origen[4] argued that the Bible should be read in several ways at once – one of these was literally, one was spiritually, one was allegorically. He said that we could not always read the Bible literally

> Once upon a time there was a very faithful and devout woman, who wanted to win the Lottery.
>
> At church on Sunday she called upon her Lord, and told him she wanted to win the Lottery.
>
> The next week, she returned to her church and spoke to her Saviour. She assured him that she knew that faith must be persistent as well as clamorous; and she accepted that he might want to test her a little first. That was all right. But now they had got that over with, could he please arrange for her to win the Lottery.
>
> By the third week she was getting a bit peevish. Enough was enough, she told him; she knew that faith could move mountains. There was nothing wrong with her faith, but she had not won the Lottery despite her enthusiastic and committed prayer. Frankly, she was somewhat disappointed. She expected better things from God and next week she had better win the Lottery or else . . .
>
> And even as she prayed there was a tremor that ran through the whole fabric of the building; there was a roll of thunder, and the roof was raised up from off the church to reveal a great light, a blinding presence. And the word of God spake unto her through that brightness in a mighty voice, saying –
>
> 'Susan. Meet me halfway. Buy a ticket.'

because some of it was literally nonsense, but it could not be read as nonsense because it was a sacred text – therefore it had to have some other meaning. (He came to this conclusion, incidentally, when he read that the Law forbade eating vultures. He decided that this was a silly law because no one could possibly be tempted to want to eat anything as disgusting as a vulture, and so the act did not need to be prohibited. Since God would not waste precious space giving pointless instructions, he decided that the text must have some other subtler, or less literal, meaning.)

We tend to forget that no one was what we would now call a 'fundamentalist' before the nineteenth century – indeed the word itself did not exist, because there was nothing to describe. I would argue that our loss of the ability to think mythically, poetically, allegorically, creatively, theologically, and *artfully* is a greater threat to our religious experience and faith than anything that good scientists have to report about the way the world actually is.

We tend also to forget that if there is something called 'fundamentalism' that tries to insist that the Bible can only be read in one way and at one level, then there is also something which should be called 'scientism'. Like fundamentalism, scientism tries to insist that everything in the world can only be read in one way, and at one level.

On the whole, it is not serious scientists who are guilty of scientism. Fred Hoyle, a physicist, once wrote: 'I have always thought it curious that while most scientists claim to eschew religion, it actually dominates their thought more than it does the clergy.'[5] I'm afraid he may be right, and I strongly suspect that most pre-Enlightenment thinkers would find our inability to think at two levels at once a proof of our stupidity or a cause for compassion.

Perhaps one of the reasons why we get into such a tangle when we try to think about the relationship between God as creator and contemporary science, is because in the sentence 'God made the world', we have focused too much on the two nouns, and not enough on the verb.

So what do we mean by 'made'? I looked this word up in the dictionary and found an enormously long entry. Not so much a long and complicated history, like some words have, but a long list of different uses for a basic and simple word. Here is a selection of these uses:

I made a cake.
I made my bed.
I made money.
I made a mistake.
I made him (do it).
I made up. (She wears make up.)
I made up to him.
I made up my mind.

I made a journey.
I made haste.
I made a face.
I made it happen.
I made him cross.
I made good time.
I made it (caught the train).
I made it (became famous).
I made do.
I made it up.
I made a friend.

It made a difference.
It made me sick.

We made peace.
We made war.
We made up.
We made music.
We made love.

(In addition – and I put this in for my own delight – the word 'poet' is derived from the Greek word ποητεσ (*poetes*) which means 'maker'.)

God made the world.
Did God force it into existence? (He made it exist.)
Did God tidy up an old mess as best he could in a hurry? (I made a bed.)
Did God measure, stir, blend together some ingredients and apply heat (as a cook would make a meal)?
Did God invent it (make it up, the way children tell lies or writers tell stories)?
This is not frivolous. Seriously, it is very serious.
It is the first thing we know about God. It is the first thing we say about God.
In the beginning God created.
In the beginning God created heaven and earth.

In the beginning God created heaven and earth and saw
that it was good.
Before God redeemed, God *made*.

God makes music?

God makes love? Not in the sense that God made love like the engineer made the car, or the mechanic made it work; but, as in good human sex, love was generated by, of, God's passionate acts; and love was God's passionate act. Bernard of Clairvaux described the Holy Spirit as 'the passionate kiss between the Father and the Son'. Or does God make the world like a loving heterosexual couple 'makes a baby'? Or indeed as a rapist makes a baby?

God is a poet, an artist? Does God make the world the way toddlers paint pictures? The early pictures of small children who are set free to paint what they want are different from adult Western pictures: they are not static. An adult asked to paint a picture of a building catching fire chooses one moment out of a story and illustrates that. Toddlers don't: they paint the fire (lots of red). Then they paint (usually on top of this) the fire engine arriving (more red); then the firemen getting out (black bits); then the hoses shooting water (general smear across the picture which is now a brownish glob, but the artists are satisfied).[6] Did God make a mess? Or a picture so intricate, so complex, so enmeshed in time, that we have the greatest difficulty in seeing what the picture is – especially as we are part of the painting. Do you remember a few years ago there were those strange computer-generated pictures ('Magic Eye') that at first glance looked like complicated multi-coloured geometric patterns, but which if you looked at them in a slightly different way, or from a different angle, suddenly revealed a clear picture of something perfectly recognizable.[7]

God made the universe (or perhaps, God makes the universe, or God is making the universe).

In order to know what this crucial sentence means – *how* God made, and even *why* God made – we had better learn *what* God made (a cake, a song, a universe, a mistake, a difference, a mess, music, love). That is why we turn to the scientists. Not because they know it all, but because they have committed themselves, so they tell us, to looking, to *looking* at what is and seeing it more and more clearly.

Natural history is not taught in seminary. This is curious, as most people in pastoral ministry are about 567 times more likely to be asked about cosmology or sub-nuclear physics or human biology or evolution than they are to be asked about irregular Greek verbs or the dangers of the patripassionist heresy. If we monotheists are going to go around claiming that our 'God made the heaven and the earth', it is not unreasonable to expect us to know something about what that heaven and earth actually *are*.

The funny thing is that, as Fred Hoyle indicated, many scientists actually do theology to quite an extraordinary degree. This may be because they have nothing to be scared of. Stephen Hawking, for example, is certainly not scared or ashamed to deal with such issues. He openly believes his science has displaced God entirely. As he puts it:

> The idea that space and time may form a closed surface without boundary has profound implications for the role of God in the affairs of the universe... So long as the universe had a beginning, we could suppose it had a creator. But if the universe really is completely self-contained, having no boundary or edge, it would have neither beginning nor end: it would simply be. What place then for a creator?[8]

None the less, looking for the scientific facts among the far-flung astral bodies, or peering at them within the whizzing orbits of the atom, seems to affect people's language – and therefore we may assume their consciousness. Elsewhere in the same book, Hawking – who can imagine no point in a creator, no place nor need for one – demands in painfully beautiful and urgent terms, which seem more reminiscent of the Spanish mystics than of deductive logic, 'What is it that breathes fire into the equations and makes a universe for them to describe?'[9]

It is questions like this one, more the imperialist ambitions of science, that have made a dialogue between science and theology fashionable again.

And have Christians said 'thank you'?

From the theological point of view, science has become approachable again. While the Newtonian (or Enlightenment) myth of a 'knowable' mechanistic universe, which could best be understood by being broken down into ever-smaller component parts, dominated the Western imagination, there was very little that theology could say. If we believe that we have a clockwork universe, we can still believe in God, but a clockmaker God is a pretty boring God. There is not a lot you can say about a God who does nothing much except wind the whole show up and then sit around for eternity waiting for it to wind down again (or go wrong).

Some theologians dealt with this difficulty by pointing out the things that scientists couldn't explain, and trying to use these gaps in human knowledge as a proof of God. The trouble is that as scientists got better and better at explaining things, this God of the Gaps got smaller and smaller, and indeed less and less interesting.

I used the word myth ('the Newtonian myth') quite carefully. The most reductionist and mechanistic of these scientists still thought that the pursuit of truth was not *just* important in itself, but that their description, their story about an orderly and comprehensible universe, offered a new freedom – freedom from anxiety and slavery. When Napoleon asked one of the leading rationalist philosophers of his time, Pierre-Simon Laplace, about the place for God in this new scientific universe, Laplace is supposed to have answered, 'I have no need of that hypothesis.' But in a gentler frame of mind he also wrote: 'Supposing that this being [an intelligent human] were in a position to analyse all events then nothing would be uncertain for him, and both future and past would be open to him.'

We would at last be free from fear, safe from the terror

that flies by night. Given the extraordinary optimism, energy, and arrogance of this sort of science; given that Christianity had already failed – since Galileo – to find a vocabulary to incorporate scientific developments, it is not surprising that theology simply withdrew from the struggle to find a huge God in the whole universe. It retreated, locating a much smaller but apparently impregnable God in the interior life and a spiritualized private moralism – which has been described as 'ethics tinged with emotion'. It is not surprising either, though worth thinking about, that the things of the Spirit were increasingly handed over to *women* (who didn't, it was then believed, have the right sort of brains to do science). At the same time, women were more and more firmly shut up within the home – guardians of the domestic shrines since the intellectual ones had been closed down.

But recently science has started to paint a rather different picture. The science of the twentieth century has, at least at the imaginative level (and, it has to be said, to the appalled fury of many of the best scientific minds), reopened the floodgates. Quantum mysticism is trendy; cosmology is chic; psychology and genetics are gossip; the mass media see science as a popular topic; science fiction, in novels, films, and other art forms, is massively popular.

Religious people ought to be well placed to join in this open-eyed and open-hearted investigation. One reason for this is that our 'safety' is located elsewhere (or should be). We have less need of scientific certainty and reassurance. Start with 'God exists' and everything we can learn will tell us more about God. Or, as Paul Davies puts it, 'It is often said that you cannot prove the existence of God. Yet science does have value in theological debate because it gives us new concepts that sometimes make popular notions of God untenable.'[10]

So let us try to look at what some of the sciences are presently saying.

Mathematics

There are a number of things that are darkly strange about mathematics.

Why is it, for example, that the only people who 'like' maths are the people who are good at 'doing' maths? This is odd. With most human endeavours there are people who like to admire and enjoy the achievements of others. If you think about music or painting or writing, you become aware that lots of people like to go to concerts, play records, and listen to the radio who can't 'play' an instrument; that art galleries are full of interested visitors who never even try to paint or sculpt; and that it is perfectly acceptable to enjoy a novel or a poem without ever putting pen to paper yourself. It is not just art either: I avidly watch Wimbledon and Rugby League on the television, although I couldn't do a drop volley to save my life, never mind survive in a scrum. I am fascinated by mountaineering, Antarctic adventures, human psychology, medieval history, gymnastics . . . and the list goes on. I want to know about all sorts of things I cannot *do*. The same applies to sciences: I don't need to be a biologist, a chemist, or a physicist to be interested in learning about those things. Indeed, books on physics and biology topics frequently top the non-fiction bestseller lists.

But not maths. Maths is boring.

Or so we think. I have a strong feeling that many people will want to skip this section. But do give it a try, because actually mathematics is deeply mysterious and beautiful.

And it has, increasingly, deep affinities with theology. Galileo once said that 'the book of nature is written in mathematical language', and the more contemporary mathematician James Jeans went further: 'God is a mathematician.' Rationalist, logical mathematicians catch themselves referring to 'the *unreasonable* effectiveness of mathematics . . . it is probable that there is some *secret* here which remains to be discovered'. Paul Davies sums up the connection:

> Science is based on the assumption that the universe is thoroughly rational and logical at all levels. Miracles are not allowed. This implies that there should be reasons for the particular laws of nature that regulate the physical universe. Atheists claim that the laws exist reasonlessly and that the universe is ultimately absurd. As a scientist I find this hard to accept. There must be an unchanging rational ground in which the logical orderly nature of the universe is rooted. Is this rational ground like the timeless God of Augustine? Perhaps it is. But in any case the lawlike basis of the universe is a more fruitful place for a dialogue between science and theology than focusing on the origin of the universe.[11]

To understand why Davies feels that mathematical laws should be the basis of such a discussion we need to understand a bit about what maths really is (or claims to be). It is not about getting sums wrong and learning your seven times table.

Mathematics has always set itself different standards from other sciences. In the material sciences proof (a demonstration that something is true) is based on experiments. You have to show that your idea will work in practice (repeatably) in the actual physical world. The world itself is the ultimate judge of whether something is true or not. Mathematics makes a different claim – it deals not with messy old reality (matter, the world), but with pure, abstract ideas.

Try and think about what a number *is*. It is completely abstract. The number 3 cannot be separated from three-ness. Nothing in the real world is '3'; '3' is just a symbol for what certain sizes of groups of different things have in common. What is truly amazing is how quickly small children can see what 3 balls, 3 boys, 3 dots on a page, and the funny swiggly sign '3' have in common; 3 is just the agreed sign for this abstract idea.

The only way to make these odd scribbles remotely useful or meaningful is to lay down some ground rules, which say how you can play with them (for example, 2 + 2 will equal 4). However, if these rules can't be proved to be complete and consistent with one another, the pure logic of the whole game breaks down – because, unlike other sciences, you are not allowed to prove this just by experiment. Even a simple little rule, like 8 + 1 will always equal the same as 1 + 8, becomes a leap of faith. In fact, in 'real life' we know that this is often not true: when getting dressed in the morning we know that the order in which we add socks and shoes to our body makes a very noticeable difference to the end result.

Now this would not matter much if maths were just an intellectual game (with lots of games there are particular 'house rules', and so long as everyone agrees with them the game can continue quite happily with all sorts of variations). The problem is that mathematics is bizarrely (unreasonably) effective in describing the real actual world – or, to be precise, in predicting what you will find if you look in the real actual material world.

A very good example of this came up in the first half of the nineteenth century. In 1781 William Herschel had become the first named person in recorded history to discover a planet – now called Uranus. He found it the way you might expect, the way most things are discovered, by looking, just by looking at everything through his home-made telescope. He looked and looked and thought about what he saw, and he discovered a planet. (Planets don't twinkle like stars, but – under sufficient magnification – show a disk rather than a point of light and they move through the sky independently.)

After he had established that it was there, other astronomers tried to plot its orbit; but wherever they thought it ought to be, it wasn't. They worked out therefore that it was being pulled out of its expected orbit by the gravitational force of another invisible planet, somewhere out there, somewhere beyond the known limits of the sun's system. In 1845 a young *mathematician* (with no astronomical practice) called John Couch Adams worked out by maths alone exactly where it was. Fairly typically, he could not persuade any astronomers to get out of bed and look for it. Another mathematician, a

> M. Eiffel, an eminent French engineer of the nineteenth century, proposed to build a Tower for the Grand Exhibition in Paris. His plans were not moderate: the tower would be the last word in contemporary engineering – it would involve 15,000 steel girders, and over seven million threaded rods, held in place by two and a half million bolts. It would be the tallest structure ever built in Europe (the previous claimant to this glory was Lincoln Cathedral spire, which had fallen down more than three hundred years before). It would be so tall and so delicately constructed that it would actually weigh less than the cylinder of air that encompassed it. It would be tous qu'il y a de chic and modernity.
>
> He drew up the plans. The exhibition committee was keen. A site by the Seine, at the bottom of the Champ de Mars, was selected; subscriptions were raised. Then Monsieur E. hit a substantial snag: no construction company would build it for him. It was held that an erection over 700 feet high was scientifically impossible and probably blasphemous as well. It would fall down and their souls, together with their professional reputations and their pocket books, would be put at risk.
>
> There is something intrepid and unstoppable about many of those high Victorian engineers. Eiffel was no exception: undaunted, he became his own site foreman and advertised up and down the length of rural France for acrobats and tightrope walkers; circus professionals who could, he thought, understand his vision and have the nerve to act it out.
>
> He was right. We see the result still, the epitome of Paris, serene, elegant, bold, floating over the river and displayed on several million postcards.
>
> The Eiffel Tower was built by acrobats and tightrope walkers; engineers and philosophers of balance; artists of the body.

Frenchman called Leverrier, came up with the same sums and the same location the following year. Eventually, someone pointed their telescope where they had been told to, and there it was, not twinkling but glowing, sea-blue and tiny, exactly where this abstract game called mathematics had said that it would be. This planet was Neptune. The same thing keeps on happening: for example, Einstein proves mathematically, however improbably, that light bends under the force of gravity and when someone finally works out a way to test this experimentally, there is light bending.

So this formal, abstract game of number manipulation corresponds in some deeply tricky way to material, measurable reality.

Now for centuries this did not matter. It did not matter because, up until the beginning of the nineteenth century, people believed that mathematics very simply was related to the real world. Mathematics was a set of universal rules that applied at all times and on all occasions. The foundation to all maths was Euclid[12] and his geometry. Euclid had worked out his rules (axioms) for geometry experimentally, like ordinary sciences. Legend taught that he drew diagrams in the sand and worked out principles to explain what it was and was not possible to draw. It was on this basis of what could be drawn – what 'theories' could be demonstrated in the real world – that Euclid's geometry was founded: it was real, it was solid, it was necessarily true.

These principles, this sort of maths, were accepted throughout the Western world more or less universally. They did more than underpin mathematical research, they were also widely influential in developing moral and legal codes, and ideas about government, art, and human behaviour (early psychology). This remained the case for a remarkably long time. For example, Kant's philosophy was founded on Euclid's geometry. In order to know or understand anything, Kant believed, there have to be some things that are *necessarily* and always and everywhere true.

For Kant, as for most thinking people before the nineteenth century, the way we were as human beings, the way our brains were constructed, *guaranteed* that we would find Euclid's system solidly and unshakeably true.

However, during the nineteenth century mathematicians began to find circumstances in which Euclid's geometry did not work; it was not inevitably – always, everywhere – true. There were better models. There were other – and more useful – geometries. For example, Euclid's theories assume that all space is flat. In flat space, of course, parallel lines never meet and the three internal angles of a triangle always add up to 180 degrees. But not all space is flat.

Actually, sailors of course had known this for a very long time: navigation is impossible without a geometry that works on a curved surface because that is what the sea has. In spherical geometry, for example, the angles of a triangle do not always add up to 180 degrees – but, apparently, they had considerately spared mathematicians and philosophers this painful knowledge! As the book *Longitude* demonstrated so clearly, an intellectual elite can be so patronizing towards practical solutions that it simply will not realize or accept the existence of these solutions or their consequences.[13]

But during the nineteenth century the mathematicians and philosophers began to catch up with the seafarers and merchants. Long before 1915, when Einstein proved mathematically and conclusively that space was curved, mathematicians had suspected this. In curved plane geometry parallel lines can meet and triangles get up to all sorts of tricks. These discoveries undermined idealist thinking about the world in a profound way; and it opened up the floodgates of modern relativism – the philosophy that says nothing is demonstrably true in all and every circumstance. (An idea that philosophers have come round to, but that the Church continues to deplore.)

Bernard Shaw, with his usual aggressive vigour, described the mathematical situation at the end of the nineteenth century like this:

> Geometry, throughout the seventeenth and eighteenth centuries, remained, in the war against empiricism, an impregnable fortress of the idealists. Those who held – as was generally held on the continent – that certain knowledge, independent of experience, was possible about the real world, had only to point to geometry: none but a madman they said would throw doubt on its validity and none but a fool would deny its objective reference.[14]

But by the time Shaw wrote this, the fortress had been conquered. Many mathematicians fled in exile from the 'real world' and increasingly came to see maths in a highly 'formal' way. It was like art rather than like science. It was a creation, an invention, of the highest intellectual capacities of the human mind. It needed no reference to the outside world (mean, nasty, brutish, and short); it remained in and of itself a pure and beautiful construct of perfect reason: a head game, but a lovely one. (I think this explains the bizarre arrogance that one sometimes hears, even now, from mathematicians. I asked one once what the difference was between maths and physics. The answer I got was, 'If it's for anything then it isn't maths.' This seems to treat maths as contemplatives sometimes treat prayer – both are risky places to live.)

Anyway, the poor old mathematicians' troubles had hardly started. By the turn of the twentieth century these formalists, as they are called, would have appeared to have won, at least within the rarefied world of mathematicians. They beat the retreat from the real world and the troops either deserted (to become physicists) or followed the leaders. (A similar process to the one we saw, in the last chapter, that took place in the relationship between theology and science during the same period.)

This meant that they all basically agreed that all mathematics could be regarded as the formal logical manipulation of symbols based on agreed rules (these mathematical rules are called axioms). The only things that were needed to make the whole game seamless were some axioms (rules) that were complete and consistent. The mathematicians needed a method for deciding, in a limited number of steps, whether any particular mathematical statement was true or false.

In 1900, the Second International Conference for Mathematicians was held in Paris (which had incidentally been rearranged to fall in the opening year of the new century – an oddly sentimental decision for people who had finally concluded that the 'real world' did not count). The key-note speaker, David Hilbert – instead of looking back over a very successful past century – gave a dynamic speech outlining 23 pressing mathematical questions, including this question about the truth of mathematical statements, which needed to be tackled. He was filled with a sweeping optimism: 'We hear within us the perpetual call: there is the problem. Seek its solution. You can find it by reason, for in mathematics there is no *ignorabimus* [we shall not know].'

So the mathematicians set to work and, 30 years later, with two startlingly simple (in mathematical terms) theorems, Kurt Godel demonstrated that there was a *ignorabimus*. He proved conclusively that it was mathematically impossible to prove whether any mathematical statement was complete and consistent. The first incompleteness theorem proved that there will always be relevant statements that can be neither proved nor disproved. The second incompleteness theorem made the whole situation even worse because among the unprovable statements is the statement that 'any axiom system is consistent'.

Gone for ever is the old expectation that given enough time and ingenuity any genuine mathematical problem can be solved. Before Godel there were true statements and false statements; now there is a third category, statements that cannot be proven to be either true or false.[15] They are called undecidable statements. And it turns out that there are lots and lots of them: 'Undecidable propositions run through mathematics like threads of gristle that criss-cross a steak in such a dense way that they cannot be cut out without the entire steak being destroyed.'[16]

Or, to put it another way, and as John Barrow, the mathematical historian, rather cleverly comments: 'If a religion is defined to be a system of thought which requires belief in unprovable truths, then mathematics is the only religion that can prove it is a religion.'[17]

Of course, this need not alarm any Christian, since, as we have seen, Christianity has always taught that the infinite could not be proven by any philosophical system (which is what mathematical logic is). But it is exciting to think that when the mathematical laws that shape the universe were laid down, they revealed in their complex depths exactly what is also revealed in the Scriptures and the traditions of the Church.

As a matter of fact, this correspondence between mathematics and theology occurs elsewhere as well. My personal favourite example is Georg Cantor's proof that infinities come in different sizes. There are larger and smaller infinities.

This is totally counter-intuitive. Think about it.

I find it an extraordinarily provocative and delightful idea. I have to admit, though, that my delight has a personal element: Cantor's 'proof' was the first mathematical theory that I felt I understood. I do not mean the first that I *believed* (I would happily accept the authority of the mathematical community on such matters), but that imaginatively (though not mathematically) I could follow the argument: I could grasp both the problem and the solution. It was for me a breakthrough – I went around grinning like a maniac for several days and was so pleased with myself that I even had a character in the novel I was writing at the time explain the whole thing to her sister.[18]

Earlier I quoted Hoyle saying that while most scientists claim to eschew religion, it actually dominates their thoughts to a surprising degree. Nowhere is this more true than when it comes to infinities. Scientists love infinity – unlike most theologians, who tend to shy away from the infinite and come swiftly home to ethics and immanence. Mathematicians love infinities, even 'soft' scientists like economists love infinities because it makes their work so much more elegant. Going from the 'very large' to the infinite is a bit like stepping back from a television screen: once you are far enough away, the indecipherable complexity of the large number of light dots resolves itself into a coherent picture.

Cantor showed mathematicians how they could play in the world of the infinite. It was the loveliest treasure he brought back from his adventure into the world of Set Theory (which now underpins the way maths is taught in primary schools). Mathematicians were so excited by Cantor's work that their rigour collapsed into lyrical and ecstatic prose: Bertrand Russell described Cantor's achievement as 'possibly the greatest of which the world can boast'. And Hilbert boasted that 'from the paradise created for us by Cantor, no one will drive us out'.[19]

Most infinities are the same size as each other – that is to say, the items in one infinity can be paired off with the items in another. Initially, all Cantor did was demonstrate that the 'Power Set' (i.e. the set consisting of all the subsets) of an infinite set was larger than the infinite set (because it includes itself). In 1969 another mathematician developed Cantor's work to prove that *infinities come in an infinite number of sizes*. This means that:

> We cannot know Cantor's Absolute [the mathematical name for the largest possible infinity] or any other Absolute by rational means, for any Absolute being a unity and hence complete within itself, must include itself . . . If it is One, then it is a member of itself and thus can only be known through a flash of mystical vision . . . We are barred from ultimate knowledge, from ultimate explanation, by the very rules of reasoning that prompt us to seek such an explanation in the first place. If we wish to progress beyond, we have to embrace a different concept of 'understanding' from that of rational explanation.[20]

Thus Cantor's Absolute is a perfect image for what we experience of God. When I speak of a Big Enough God I am not merely thinking of an Infinite God, but of the God of infinities, the Absolute, which either chooses to reveal itself or remains veiled in mystery. Modern mathematics does begin to feel like the language that God talks.

Nor need we fear, as I think we have a tendency to do, that 'hard' scientific knowledge will strip away beauty any more than it will explode and destroy mystery. It is the hardest maths after all that have discerned the order and beauty of chaos itself; in, for instance, the bizarrely orderly swirls of the Mandelbrot sets, which replicate across scale and reveal pattern that shapes branches and leaves and waves and grass in the wind. Increasingly, mathematicians recognize the role that beauty – usually called 'elegance' – plays in the discernment of truth:

> The mathematician's patterns, like the painter's or the poet's, must be beautiful, the ideas like the colours or the words must fit together in a harmonious way. Beauty is the first test: there is no permanent place in the world for ugly mathematics . . . It may be very hard to define mathematical beauty, but that is just as true as beauty of any kind – we may not know quite what we mean by a beautiful poem, but that does not prevent us from recognising one.[21]

What Keats said about art, 'Beauty is truth, truth beauty', and Isaiah said about theology, 'Beautiful on the Mountains are the feet of them that bring good news', is the same thing as mathematicians are saying about their own work.

I find the exploration of mathematics, even though I know that I will never do more than peek over the high wall into the lovely garden, deeply pleasing. It has become for me a source of joy and a code, or even a language, that enables me to think about God.

It is also the mother tongue for physics, the contemporary science that has most directly challenged Christian orthodoxies and complacencies.

Once upon a time there was a couple who were married. And since the time in question was about now, they had the usual chronic argument about the housework. He felt his job was very important and required his best attentions – and that, as she was at home with their children, she had plenty of time to see to everyone's material needs.

(Oh, I forgot to mention that he was a parish priest.)

She felt that this was not fair.

(Been there? Remember, it is not just about gender. Martha and Mary had the same fight, and Mary even got Jesus on her side. Actually it is mainly about gender.)

One day this priest went to a far country to study more about his God; and there he saw a kind of poverty he had not had to deal with before, and a kind of Christlike dignity he had not had to deal with before.

He came home full of the spirituality of the little moment; the dignity of manual labour; the bias to the poor; and the liberation gospel of Jesus Christ.

He cleaned and he scrubbed and he cooked and he toiled and he vacuumed and he shopped and he washed up, and he washed up and he washed up.

One day his wife said, 'How come that when he does the washing up it's theology; and when I do the washing up it's the washing up?'

The big and the little (the huge and the tiny)

The job of physics is to describe how things are – or, rather, the physical forces and powers that make things how they are.

Once upon a time this description could be obtained by practical experiment. Heat up some liquid and see what happens – does it change colour, expand, contract, disappear, solidify, vaporize, affect the things next to it? You can look (and smell, touch, listen, taste) and see what the effect of heat *is*. Do it often enough and attentively enough and you may be able to come up with a theory or general 'law' about heat (e.g. it can't pass from a cooler body to a hotter one). Then you can think of different situations and experiments by which you can test this theory and see if it holds good, and under what circumstances. Then, if you are conscientious, you can ask a whole lot of other people to do the same experiment, or any others they can think of, to test your theory – just to make sure that you hadn't done something stupid, or biased, or inattentive. This is called the scientific method.

It was physical. You are Newton, you are sitting under a tree in your orchard – probably, if you are Newton, dreaming about alchemy and other semi-magical and deeply metaphysical matters – when an apple drops on your head. This makes you think about why apples drop on heads. You think of gravity; you test it out; it works. It turns out to be a theory of wide-ranging usefulness; it explains a great number of things as well, like planetary orbits.

But nowadays you can sit in your orchard for a very long time. Neither a sub-atomic particle nor a black hole is going to drop on your head. (It is in fact physically possible to 'see' some sub-atomic particles very, very briefly. You go to Switzerland to the CERN LEP[22] accelerator – which rather pleasingly runs in a vast artificial circular cavern underneath the Villa Deodati where Mary Shelley wrote *Frankenstein*. Here scientists accelerate matter almost to the speed of light and watch on detector screens for 'accidents' to happen: for particles to smash into each other so fast that they fragment. Particles fly out and if the scientists are lucky, they may, just for a moment so fleeting that it cannot be seen, capture an 'ill defined smear' or even an 'event': a sub-nuclear particle being destroyed, and displaying its death on a recording screen. But this is not the sort of physical physics that gave the science its original 'matter of fact' authority.)

The big has got too big and the small too small for sight, for description, even perhaps for imagination. Culturally we use the word 'million' almost casually. Meanwhile, we worry that after 2,000 years the imagery of Christianity is no longer capable of describing our so different lives.

There have not been one million days since the crucifixion; and contemporary physics requires us to think in terms of millions of millennia or millionths of seconds. This probably does not worry God. God's time-scale is preposterous; from the stand-point of eternity all this is but drops in an ocean. And it need only worry us if we are arrogant enough to believe that we have to know what is going on in order to feel safe, *and* that we have a right to feel safe. What we do have to understand and accept – and learn to rejoice in – is that we cannot trust our physical senses, we cannot know only that which we can experience, and that we cannot grasp the enormity of God's creation – and therefore presumably the enormity of God's love. Physics, and its mysterious mathematical laws, bridges the gap.

The universe that physics is currently describing for us turns out to be extremely odd. Let us look first at the big end of the scale; at what cosmological and astronomical[23] physics are telling us about space and time and the beginning of both. The story goes a bit like this:

Once . . . not once upon a *time* exactly, because there was no time, but once upon an event. (So much was it 'once' that we call this 'event' a 'singularity', though it was/is/will be not the only singularity. A singularity is a non-place – since there is no space there is no location – of such density (although there is nothing in it) that the laws of physics don't apply, except that all the following events occur necessarily according to the laws of physics.) Without 'cause', this singularity suddenly expanded with enormous energy, thus generating enormous heat and enormous velocity. Obviously 'suddenly', which describes time, 'velocity', which describes time, and 'heat', which describes matter, are all a bit inaccurate here – but they will have to do, because there is nothing else. So total and fast and complete and hot and energetic was this moment that within millionths of seconds the laws of maths and physics had kicked in and the whole thing was working to such a degree of precision that it has continued to do so ever since.

Indeed it has worked to such a degree of precision that now, all this time later, there are not just human beings existing, but human beings intelligent and conscious and desperate enough to believe that the precision itself constitutes 'proof' of God. (I have to say that personally I find that reasoning dubious. Perhaps I am not desperate enough.)

The degree of precision involves bizarre details though. Professor Hawking has suggested that:

> If the density of the universe one second after the Big Bang had been greater by one part in a thousand billion, the universe would have recollapsed after ten years. On the other hand if the universe at that time had been less by the same amount, the universe would have been essentially empty since it was about ten years old.[24]

Professor Davies, looking at the balance between the outward thrust of that first moment and the inward gravitational attraction required for the universe to exist as it exists, calculates that it had to be as it is with an 'error factor' of less that one part in 10^{60}: 'Suppose you wanted to fire a bullet at a one-inch target the other side of the observable universe, twenty billion light years away. Your aim would have to be accurate to that same part in 10^{60}.'[25]

Why stop there? The plot continues as precariously in the next phase. Such an initial expansion would have generated mainly lighter gases – hydrogen and helium. They would need to be fused together, under great pressure and temperature, to generate the heavier elements like carbon, oxygen, and nitrogen. This fusing can happen in the inside of certain types of star. Periodically such stars blow up, scattering these newly made, heavier elements into space, where they can clump together to form different sorts of combinations – eventually planets (and from our point of view, eventually *this* planet, Earth, with its precise and highly improbable combination of factors which makes our specific form of life possible). Stars form through gravity squashing a cloud of gas particles together; the squashing (pressure) heats them enough for the necessary nuclear fusion to take place. If gravity were any weaker, the stars wouldn't get hot enough; if gravity were any stronger, the stars would get too big and burn out too fast.

Come in from out there for a moment. Even here on this planet, the precision and its improbability are peculiar and challenging. All substances increase in density from their gaseous form, to their liquid state, and then their solid state. This is why steam rises and most solid things sink. There is, however, an exception: H_2O. Water molecules are made up of hexagons of hydrogen atoms arranged in what is called a 'cage structure'. The consequence is that, uniquely, as they solidify (freeze), they trap air in between the molecules. This is why ice floats on water. And it is a bit of luck that it does, because if it sank, more ice would form on top of it, and then more and more and more. The whole planet would be frozen solid in next to no time.[26]

So what is going on here? A bit of luck? A very clever creator? One of an infinite series of chances? This last is the thinking behind the many worlds (or rather infinite singularities) theory. (The idea here is that if you have an infinite number of occasions and an infinite amount of time, *anything that can possibly happen* WILL *happen*. I find this very useful when trying to think about heaven, but unnecessarily far-fetched when thinking about the temporal world.)

Let us make two radical assumptions:

1 There is a God who made 'heaven and earth'.
2 The current scientific picture of how the cosmos is, is fundamentally correct. (We should hold to this with intelligence and enthusiasm; but, after all, people have been offered a whole range of such stories throughout history and they have each been replaced eventually by a more complex and more dynamic one. We have to take on trust what we are told, so as to have a functioning narrative to live within, but we must not be too ready to die for it. Nor to kill anyone who suggests an alternative.)

With these assumptions in place, what sort of God would we be talking about?

The first thing we see is a God who is greater than time. Too many of us (or too many parts of each of us) manage to conceive of God as a sort of very old magician, who existed from the beginning of time, and then – as a kind of conjuring trick – decided one morning to 'create something' and picked on the universe. St Augustine knew better: he was clear that God existed outside of time and that time was *part* of the creation, not prior to it. Current physicists would confirm this last phrase: time is not a constant, neutral field on which history plays itself out. Einstein demonstrated that time (and space) are part of the game itself, and therefore are affected by it as well as affecting it. Time can be warped, manipulated, stretched, compressed, and changed by other events.

We can also see, in this cosmos, a God of enormous intelligence and subtlety. God is smart; that is what the far-flung galaxies sing to us – a not obviously affectionate God; on the other hand, not demonstrably dictatorial either – but certainly clever. Whatever else the universe is, simple it is not. This is a God who is prepared to design in, as it were, these immensely complex, rarefied, subtle, beautiful laws of mathematics and then allow them power over what is. If God – as cosmologists demonstrate – is necessarily outside time (and space and matter) and the universe is created along such delicately precise lines, then one has to say not just that God is clever enough to 'do' these laws, but also subtle enough to keep them.

One of the arguments consistently brought to bear on the existence of God is the idea that an all-powerful God would have kept a tighter grip on what was going on. That the random, chancy nature of the way the universe is proves that there is no God, because God would have managed it all a bit more aggressively. It seems surprisingly hard for people to imagine God acting as most of us, at least for a few seconds, a few times in our lives, have acted. One can be powerful enough to do something, one can desire to do it; and one can then do it, or *choose not to do it*. The most common reason for choosing not to do what one has the power to do, and the desire to do, is recognizing the otherness and the freedom of the other. Or, put more simply, respect. What we see in the universe is God's profound respect for the universe. We see a respecting God (this is *not* the same as a loving God).

I once had a rather strange argument with Professor Atkins, the eminent Oxford University chemist. He said that God could not exist, because if God had made the world as it is he would be a very lazy God: he appeared to leave so much to abstract laws, and pure chance. Now, leave aside for the moment the very odd notion that something cannot exist because it does not have ethical practices that I approve of (I don't approve of the ethics of retro-viruses or racists, but that hardly stops them existing). Instead look at the issue of why anyone should think that not interfering was a demonstration of idleness rather than respect. I suspect it is to do with whether or not one can genuinely see *patience* as a good thing, and perhaps this is harder for scientists (who must intervene and get-on-with-it in order to do their job) than it is for artists or mothers or, say, gardeners. The God who made this universe is, rather obviously, a God who thinks on a large scale; a God who can, unlike us, think not just in millions, but in complex infinities. This God is surely a profoundly patient God, prepared to see galaxies form and die, chemical ooze hang around hopefully for millennia, information take millions of light years to arrive at a place where it can be useful, and so on. This is a God who is prepared to wait and see what will happen next. One might almost argue for a 'curious' God, but for the moment let us just note that the God who made the world we observe is a patient God. This is of course merely standard Jewish faith written in cosmic magnification – a God who is infinitely more patient with the chosen people than they are with him. (I never said that observing the works of the God of creation would produce a *different*

God from the God of revelation. One of the most annoying things about this search of mine is how often it turns out that the oldest ideas about God are the ones that the created order supports.)

So, from the reports of Big Physics (cosmology) we see the outlines of an intelligent, subtle God who is larger than the whole creation, but patient and respectful towards it.

At the heart of all this we see an expansion, an explosion, of such energy and dynamism, of such control and precision, that we must acknowledge a God who is very powerful or very creative or – most plausibly – both.

I also have a strong suspicion when I look at the universe that this powerful and creative God has made, that we can see distinct traces of a God with a sense of humour. To so elaborate the coincidences – the human body contains almost exactly the same number of cells as the Milky Way (our galaxy) contains stars. To make a solar system (ours again) in which *everything* revolves in the same direction except Triton, one of Neptune's moons, which stubbornly turns in the opposite direction. To create human beings with a capacity to believe that all this was done just so that we could exist. The whole thing is preposterously far-fetched. We can choose, I think, between an egomaniac God and a laughing God. I know where my choice lies.

So far, so good. The trouble is that when we go to the other end of the scale, to the unimaginably tiny, to the nuclear and sub-nuclear level, we get a rather different (and even more bizarre) picture. And, of course, the very big is made up of the very little: the mathematics and physics of the sub-nuclear, of the quantum level, are the instruments and language of the cosmologists. The two cannot be separated, and should not be separated. You might say that the sole difference was the point of view: the focus and attention of the observer; the scale of the map.

However, scale does matter. There is a nice story about an astronomer who got up to begin a public lecture about stars, and started with a humorous remark: 'The thing about stars,' he announced, 'is that they are really quite boring.' A voice in the audience called out: 'You'd be pretty boring from a thousand light years away too.' Very briefly – although we now accept atoms as the building blocks of matter – this belief is the very recent product of a very long debate. Aristotle believed that all matter was made up of four basic elements (earth, air, fire, and water), which were affected by two forces (gravity – which caused earth and water to sink; and levity – which caused fire and air to rise). Everything was made out of a combination of these elements affected by a balance of these forces. He also believed that matter was 'continuous' – that is, one could chop a bit of matter up smaller and smaller for ever, and one would never come up against a grain or particle of matter that could not be divided.

Aristotle's contemporary, Democritus, disagreed. He thought that matter was naturally 'grainy' – that everything was made up of tiny but indivisible lumps of matter; he called these grains 'atoms' (which means indivisible in Greek) and believed that everything was made up of large numbers of assorted kinds of atoms. Since there was no available evidence for either side, the debate wandered on rather randomly for the next couple of millennia. It was not conclusively settled in favour of the atomic theory until a paper by Einstein written in 1905, just a few weeks before the famous paper on special relativity. The odd thing here is that some people had become aware that the atom (the indivisible building block of matter) might well be divisible into yet smaller 'grains' – before they even knew conclusively that it existed at all.

It is important to remember just how new and radical atomic theory is; and therefore just how much science has been able to deliver to us in how short a time. If it wasn't for the fact that the delivering scientists would hate the phrase, I would call it a sort of 'miracle'. It is certainly a testament to collegiality, hard work, rigorous thought, and creative imagination.

It is genuinely difficult for non-scientists to keep a grip on sub-nuclear physics and (packaged with it) quantum mechanics, because what the scientists tell us is so profoundly weird, counter-intuitive, and complicated. There is also a real language problem. For instance, quarks are described as coming in six 'flavours' and each flavour has three 'colours'. But although these sound like sensory descriptions, they are not. The flavours' names have nothing to do with taste (up, down, strange, charmed, bottom, and top) and all quarks are much smaller than the wavelength of visible light and so cannot have any colour. Those of us outside the technical realm cannot have any physical sense of their reality. Nor do we yet have usable metaphors or images to help understand what we are being told. Recently, many artists have struggled to catch up, to articulate and illustrate what it means to be people who live in this sort of a world. Scientists too have engaged in the attempt both to describe the discoveries and to relate them to things we do know, but it remains extremely difficult. None the less, it is important that we try. If the scientists are right – and it is probably more straightforward to assume that they are (certainly no artist or theologian could begin to demonstrate that they aren't[27]) – they are telling us some extraordinary new things about the sort of God we have got.

Go back, for a moment, to mathematics and to Godel. Because of the highly abstract and formal nature of mathematics, Godel's incompleteness theorems, although they made things tricky for mathematicians, did not obviously undermine the mechanistic, Newtonian project of describing a knowable world. Scientists could still have faith that, by experimentation, it would be possible to discover the past and the future by knowing the present position of everything and the rules by which things moved and changed. A world that had been fixed and determined at the outset because everything, from the smallest particle of matter up to the whole cosmos, was driven by immutable laws, and these were accessible to human intelligence.

In the 1920s the emergence of quantum theory put paid to that grandiose scheme. (Note that this is less than twenty years after atoms had been agreed to exist, and even fewer since Rutherford[28] had shown that atoms had an internal structure – a positively charged nucleus around which a number of electrons orbit.) The best known expression of that mortal wound is Heisenberg's Uncertainty Principle. Heisenberg proved, to the satisfaction of almost everyone who is capable of understanding it, that, 'All measurable quantities (e.g. position, momentum, energy, time) are subject to unpredictable fluctuations in their values. This unpredictability implies that the micro-world is indeterministic.'[29]

For Newtonians, this is very bad news. And it gets worse. The Uncertainty Principle does not only mean that you cannot predict what is going to happen next, but that you cannot even describe accurately what is happening now. Heisenberg proved that the more tightly you focus on one of a pair of measurements, the vaguer the other necessarily becomes – it is impossible to state accurately both where a sub-atomic particle is *and* how fast it is going somewhere else. This is not something that we 'don't know how to calculate yet'; it is not a 'gap' in the old sense. It is something that we cannot know because of the nature of how things actually are. Speed or position; energy or time: one or the other, but not both – not now, not ever.

Let me be clear – or at least as clear as I can be.

This is true at the sub-atomic level (inside the atom). At the material level – at the level of what we can see, touch, feel, and understand through our senses; at the getting-on-

> Once upon a time I met a psychiatrist who told me in all seriousness that there was no way to distinguish between Peter Sutcliffe and William Blake – nor should there be. They both heard voices, therefore they were both delusional, therefore they were both psychotic and potentially dangerous.
>
> 'But,' I said naively, 'Sutcliffe killed people and Blake wrote about Angels.'
>
> 'Exactly,' said the psychiatrist knowingly.

with-life level – Newtonian physics and the laws of cause and effect work perfectly well. You can go on an aeroplane in safety, for instance – it won't suddenly decide that we can't know both where it is and how fast it is going somewhere else.

There is of course a very interesting and not-yet-answered scientific question about how a quantum-level Big Bang produced a Newtonian-level world. When did the uncertainty drain out and why? Most popular 'new science' books duck this question – mainly because the writers aren't sure of the answers; but that does not mean that there is no answer. It is not all necessarily shrouded in mystery for ever. This quantum stuff, despite a lot of woo-woo quantum mysticism, is scientific business, not religious mystery business.

Uncertainty does not mean a belly flop from a stable mechanistic platform into a chaotic lawless whirlpool – Heisenberg, Bohr, and their colleagues do not suggest this. The uncertainties are firmly bounded by probabilities: either the particle will leap, say, from one orbit to another, or it won't. We can't know which, but we do know it will do one or the other and we can calculate the odds. When we open the box, Schrodinger's poor abused cat will be either dead or alive – it won't have turned into a mouse.[30] This is not alchemy or magic.

None the less, in the sub-atomic world, out of which the daily world is unquestionably made, *there is no deterministic power at work.*

Many people who want to believe in God find this extremely hard to accept. But it is not a failure of God, but a failure of ours: of our nerve, our imagination, our language.

Instead of determinism, there is randomness and chance. (Instead of determinism, there is freedom.)

Random chance, like determinism, shapes how the world will be tomorrow, but it does it quite differently.

In a deterministic universe, time is just the unfolding, the unrolling, the reading, of an already completed scroll, on which everything for ever has been written. (You may not know what that future will be, but there is absolutely nothing you can do to alter it.)

In a random universe – or, rather, in the specific sort of random universe that we are living in (presumably there could be other sorts) – in *this* random universe, matter (things) is at high risk. Particles are generated, flash, and die in dots of time too small for us to conceive of. (In fact, some of them die *before* they are created: this is called reverse time and it is impossible to conceive of since thoughts cannot think backwards, only forwards, in time.) In this random universe time is a force, an active creative force, and we cannot predict what it will do. It is a force, like gravity or magnetism, that creates and participates in change, in the coming into existence of completely new things. New things happen whose causes are not just 'are not known', but are not existent until chance brings them into existence.

There is no north of the North Pole.

There is no 'before the Big Bang'.

There is no cause of random events.

If this is how it is – and it seems more confusing and cowardly to argue the case than to accept it – then there are consequences for theology. It was these consequences that Einstein would not accept. 'The Old Man does not throw dice,' he insisted.[31] Yet here, in the quantum world, and therefore in the world that we know about, God does throw dice. God is a gambler. There is risk at the heart; and God, braver than we tend to be, consents to that risk. God has built risk in, has created things in this way. This means that not merely at the moral and individual level, but at the cosmic level, the creation can participate in its own creativity.

God, of course, may still be unmoved and almighty (omnipotent), but in the great act of creation at least this is not the characteristic of God that God chooses to reveal. Either we have a God who is more generous, more responsive, than we have recognized, or we have one who is not powerful or sensible at all; in which case, why bother?

So if the contemplation of space shown to us by contemporary cosmology suggests an intelligent, subtle (and witty) God, who is infinitely larger than the whole creation but patient and respectful towards it, then the contemplation of sub-nuclear physics adds richness to the picture.

We have a God who is extraordinarily generous. This God did not just create matter in order to enslave it or, in a more contemporary language, in order to manage it; but created it as a gift to itself. In the random behaviour of sub-atomic particles we see that God has really given the creation, not just lent it. God is not going to ask for it back exactly as we received it and, like a strict landlord, refuse to return our deposit. God says, 'It's yours.' It is given in the sense that we, not just *Homo sapiens* but all created matter, are not just allowed – but *obliged* – to create it, to make genuinely new things, new possibilities, within it and out of it. It is an interactive programme.

Here is a God who prefers freedom and choice to determinism, safety, and control.

We see a God who is profoundly responsive; who will proceed with the eternal task of creation, incorporating into that mighty work every possibility that the creation can come up with. We see a God who invites participation and co-operation.

We can also see a God who values difference, who does not want everything to be the same and stay the same. In one sense, we could have seen this God in the very fact of creation – that an eternal spirit should choose to create time and matter suggests that this spirit enjoys variety. Any God who consents to the number of different forms of insect life that we have on this tiny planet clearly prefers variety to smooth administration. Any God who is a unity, and chooses to be that unity in three persons, is a God who likes difference. But the God who can 'cope' with random chance as the bottom line, and delight in whatever it throws up, obviously puts a very high, and perhaps an unexpected, value on variation, innovation, and the changes that time creates.

More tentatively, I feel that here we can learn about an unknowable God. The sub-atomic level reveals to us things that are matter but that we cannot describe through our senses in the normal way. We are forced to use analogies, poetry, language we know isn't 'true' (and certainly isn't scientifically true), as we saw with the flavours and the colours of the quarks. If we recognize that there are things in the world that we cannot perceive with our senses or describe with our words, then we may become less frightened of the unknowability of God. Perhaps this might help us to become less determined to pin God down to our own definitions and images; and more willing to accept that God, quite simply, is not 'just like us'. God's sub-atomic workings are incomprehensible – random, unsettled, changing, unpredictable, wild, risky, and indescribable.

Human beings are surprisingly good at being scared. (It is what we are best at actually: perhaps, if we were not so arrogant, we should have called ourselves *Homo soppiens*, rather than *sapiens*.) In relation to all this science, Christians, along with other religious people, seem to have developed two particular fears:

1 'They' are stripping all the mystery out of everything and leaving no place for God, or poetry, or art, or love, or beauty.
2 'They' are making it all too mysterious and weird and complicated and I can't feel safe.

We can't have *both* these fears. Well, actually we can and we do, but it is patently not very intelligent of us. Furthermore, I honestly don't believe we need to have either of them. What has the new understanding of science taken away from us?

We have lost a knowable world.

We have lost a God we can pin down and bully.

We have lost a God who would pin down and bully us.

We have lost a clear role (or function or job) for God.

We have lost (or should have) a fair degree of arrogance (God, it turns out, is smarter than us).

And in exchange, all there is on offer is a wild uncertainty and a God who seems prepared to let the whole thing go its chaotic and random way.

But I am certain that in accepting this randomness, really accepting it, embracing it fearlessly, we will gain more than we lose.

We will gain complexity, freedom, and loveliness.

We will gain a universe so extraordinary that we can live giddy with awe.

We will gain the opportunity to encounter a God so magnificently creative and intelligent that we can have total confidence that whatever the 'gameplan' is (or even if there isn't one), it is in competent hands. (Any God who can 'do' complementarity can surely manage something easy like 'the resurrection of the body and the life everlasting'.)

Of course I know there are problems. There remains the central problem, which is untouched by all my scientific enthusiasms. *How* can a God – absolute, complete, pure spirit, eternal, and all-powerful – create a contingent, evolving universe, imperfect, changing universe? And not just how, but *why*?

Seriously, I don't know.

I don't know, but I hardly have time to be too bothered, given the extraordinary universe in which we live. And, oddly enough, quantum physics has offered the world a language to describe the way that two things can be incompatible, but not contradictory. It is called Bohr's theory of complementarity:

> The language of quantum theory is precise but tricky. Quantum theory does not state that something – like light for instance – can be wave-like and particle-like *at the same time*. According to Bohr's Complementarity, light reveals either a particle-like or a wave-like aspect

> depending on the context (i.e. the experiment). It is not possible to observe both the wave-like aspect and the particle-like aspect in the same situation. *However, both these mutually exclusive aspects are needed to understand 'light'*. In this sense light is both particle-like and wave-like.[32]

'God is light', we have said traditionally. So it is a happy chance that this new understanding about light should be available to help us to accept a God who is all-powerful *and* self-sacrificing. A God who is eternal, above and beyond the world of time, purely spirit, unmoved, untouched, omnipotent (and some more things that add up to the classical definition of God as 'transcendent'), and here, present in history, loving, desiring, being with, involved in, part of the created order ('immanent' or, in biblical terms, Emmanuel). A God who is three persons *and* one God.

> Creation carries on with an intricacy unfathomable and apparently uncalled for. The first ping into being of the first hydrogen atom *ex nihilo* was so unthinkable, so violently radical, that surely it should have been enough, more than enough. But look what happens. You open the door and all heaven and hell breaks loose.[33]

Home on the Range

If what we have looked at so far is 'the big picture', what might we see if we start looking on a different scale, or with a tighter focus? Now I am going to look at this planet, or mainly a tiny fraction of it – in particular, its life forms, which, so far as we know, are unique to it. And of course especially, and particularly, at the one minority life form on which we might expect to be experts – our own life form. Do we see here the same God of the whirling spaces, the risk and generosity and wildness that is carrying on 'out there'?

In one way it is far easier to think about what is going on here, because when it comes to the human sciences it is easier to check out what they are saying. We ourselves are the data, the experimental material, the objects under the microscope. So we can test the speculations and conclusions these scientists present us with. 'Does this make sense?' I can properly ask. 'Does this satisfy me? Does this accord with my experience of myself and of my fellow human beings?' Of course, we have to keep on tiptoe, alert to the possibility of self-delusion, wish fulfilment, denial, and lies; but in the end, there are some criteria of common sense that I can apply:

Does the fish soar to find the ocean;
The eagle stoop to find the air
That we ask the stars in motion
If they have tidings of thee there.[1]

This testing of grandiose theories is always a good idea – so long as you have a legitimate access to the material. For example, I don't have a particle accelerator, but I do know quite a lot of humans (Western, twenty-first-century ones primarily, I admit). Elaine Morgan, in her amusing and helpful book *The Descent of Woman*, suggests that we should test out some of the wilder claims of socio-biologists (like Morris and Ardrey) by applying their sweeping generalizations to actual examples. 'Man is the most sophisticated predator in the known universe, and uses killing as the primary way of settling disputes' has a grand sweep and persuasive sound to it. However, it sounds completely different as soon as you apply it: 'My grocer is the most sophisticated predator in the known universe'; 'My child's primary school teacher uses killing as her main way of settling disputes'. If you insert 'I', it becomes different again: 'I am the most sophisticated killer in the known universe' sounds like a child boasting in the playground.

But although it should be easier to look at ourselves than at a black hole, it can also be a lot scarier. There are two reasons for this odd fact:

1 We can describe the first few seconds of the universe, but we do not yet have a satisfactory 'description', a working model, of what makes a person; nor of what consciousness is, nor of how it works. There is profound disagreement among both the experts and among the subjects of their studies (people).
2 We are rather more personally involved in the results. It may be difficult to understand what is going on out there. It may be hard to accept it. We may not really want a God of risk and chance. Most of us would infinitely prefer (at least some of the time) a bossy nanny God who would order our every movement and keep us safe, though infantilized. But we can just about cope with it – so long as it doesn't involve *me*. I need to believe that I am different. I am the audience, not the

> show. I am just passing through. My 'true' self is spiritual; my body is a temporary (if rather messy) hotel; heaven is my real home.

That is what I would like: unfortunately, this is not true.

The best comfort we can find – and it only works on good days – is that we *cannot* lose by gaining knowledge. We have a God who is both a God of truth and of revelation. The more truth (about *anything at all* since God made it all) we can find out and embrace, the more about God we will be able to learn.

The key question here is: what am I?

Let me put the problem simply. There is a perfectly common, normal, healthy feeling that 'I' do in fact exist in time. I am the same me as I was when I was two years old. Something began when I was born and it has carried on for 50-odd years. But what is this something? It is not physical – all the cells I started with have died. It is not intellectual: all my ideas have changed (some of them frequently). It seems to have something to do with memory. But when I meet people without 'proper' memory (just as when I meet a person with some other sort of amputation, or physical loss) I do not feel that the person has been destroyed or transformed into something else: the person is still there. And in any case, we don't really know what memory is. How does it work? Where is it located? We know that it is chancy and erratic and

> Once upon a time there were two people and they loved each other.
>
> So then there were two lovers, and there was the love of the two lovers.
>
> That love was a brand new thing, that the lovers' loving made.
>
> Before they were lovers there was their love – or else they could not have been lovers.
>
> But the lovers made love – their love could not exist before they loved.

highly selective. There is something very strange about this whole business of being a person, a self.

There are two general answers to this mystery.

The traditional answer was that the 'real' self is an immortal soul. This takes up temporary residence in a human body and after it has finished with that body it will move on to the next thing (possibly developed for good or bad, but basically unchanged by its experiences). This soul is eternal, indestructible, and infinitely superior to the illusory body.[2]

The other answer is that our sense of being something more than just an assembly of material bits only goes to prove how sophisticated these bits are. We think we are souls because we have evolved such brilliant neural networks (or genetic make-ups, or chemical fluxes, or a combination of all of these). In exact opposition to the people who say we are *really* 'pure' spirit and everything else is a dream, such thinkers argue that we are *really* 'pure' matter and everything else is a delusion.[3]

Neither of these is truly satisfying.

This whole area is often called the 'mind/brain question'. I don't very much like this expression, because I have a sneaking feeling that the issue of 'mind' or 'personhood' may have something to do with bodies, not just with single organs – with the way, as human beings, we get information in (through the senses) and put it out (through language and other gestures). But I have no doubt at all that this question of 'what is a person' is going to be one of the major and most exciting areas of both science and philosophy in the twenty-first century. It will be helpful if theologians can find a useful role to play too. Perhaps by the end of the century our ideas about this will have changed as radically as our ideas about what 'matter' is and how it works changed during the last century. It is a very important question and we should want to keep up to date on such a vital matter – which affects how we feel about, and treat, other human beings, the planet, and ourselves.

I believe, then, that here, as with outer space, we should

look carefully at what the various scientists are saying and see what that reveals about God.

The sciences in this area are somewhat confused and overlapped; and our knowledge about them tends to be inadequate and contradictory. Taken together, they do not add up to a coherent picture. So my divisions here are rather arbitrary, but I am going to try and look briefly at the present state of play on intelligence, evolution, psychology, and psychiatry, and also the social sciences. The idea, as it was when I looked at the hard sciences, is to ask what sort of God might have made this sort of thing? How does this square with traditional Christian teaching about God and about us?

Intelligence

The fact of the matter is that human beings are not very bright. They have a great number of problems that they do not know how to solve. And they have an even greater number of problems that they know perfectly well how to solve, but don't for various idiotic reasons.

The fact of the matter is that human beings are very bright indeed. They have, for example, developed a remarkable capacity for applying theoretical knowledge to practical problems: their greatest achievements lie in the field of engineering and music making.

Which of these paragraphs is true?

Who is asking?

What is certainly true is that, collectively and culturally, human beings (especially in the developed world) are immensely arrogant about their intelligence – and immensely afraid of it.

There is probably a wider range of 'intelligence' within our species than any other biological quality (colour, height, dexterity, etc.). In fact, it is fascinating how readily we accept this, and how little we like to talk about it. To say 'I am taller than you' is regarded as simply descriptive; to say 'I'm more intelligent than you' is considered tasteless boasting. We are often very fearful of intelligences that fall outside the mean, in either direction: our social treatment of those at the bottom end of the IQ range is disgraceful, but we are equally suspicious of those who are 'too clever'. We like being an intelligent species, but we are rather scared of intelligent individuals. 'Be good, sweet maid, and let who will be clever' is a very strange proverb from a species that claims that it is intelligence that distinguishes our species from other species.

In 1819, a scandalous novel was published: *Frankenstein: A Modern Prometheus*. The novel has a curious status – its author, Mary Shelley, is perhaps the only individual – that is, named person – who has genuinely created a major myth. Myths (primary stories that affect thought and behaviour) usually emerge out of an 'anonymous' cultural pool,[4] often with religious origins. One of the points about them is that we do not know exactly who or where they come from. They have to come from no one's brain so that they can belong to and be claimed by everyone.

Mary Shelley did not set out consciously to 'write a myth'. She wrote a novel, roughly in the Gothic horror vein, which was going down well in Britain just then, especially in the circles she moved in. She wrote it as an entertaining game for a house party in a self-catering villa in Switzerland, stuck inside because of the worst summer weather ever recorded in Europe. She may well have written it to score points off her husband and his clever friends. But whatever her intention, she invented a character and a morality which have had an enduring influence for nearly two centuries. She invented a new sort of book – science fiction – which is now one of the best-selling genres in the world. And she outlined a primary story that, from the comic book to the nightmare, we use to express and nurture and shape our fears of our own intellectual capabilities.

The core story runs like this: a very clever and promising man[5] becomes excited at the idea of power. So he 'interferes with nature'. (You might think that in learning to read, or even getting dressed in the morning, he had already done this, but that doesn't count.) He tries to 'make life', by the application of advanced technology/ scientific knowledge. He is 'successful' – because he is very clever – but the results are disastrous.

As a matter of fact, I think that *Frankenstein* is an extraordinarily fine novel, and one about all sorts of things other than this crude outline. The 'monster' has an extremely delicate moral sensibility and is not the drooling hulk of malice that we too often think we remember. Moreover, Shelley was 'on to' something that needed articulating, about pride, about men and women, about having babies. It is also clear, as she warned, that we are not very good at looking at the potential consequences of many of the technologically advanced things that we do.[6]

But here I want to look at the effect of the story on how we think about cutting-edge scientific knowledge and the people whose intelligence delivers this to us. And this effect has been astonishing. Not many philosophical novels by dangerously radical teenage mothers written 200 years ago get referred to in tabloid headlines.

Mary Shelley did clearly articulate something that was going to grow and develop and, to some extent, come to dominate popular thinking. All robots, all artificial intelligence, and – more sadly – all attempts to describe in 'mechanical terms' the ways our own intelligence might work, are perceived as highly alarming; deeply frightening. Religious faith that ought to have helped people deal with their fear has abrogated its responsibility, by sticking to an outdated language of 'spirituality' and 'souls' and 'leaving it in God's hands'. Thus rejecting God's endless and generous offers, clearly laid out in the history of the universe, in the revelation of the creation, to treat us as grown-ups.

This is slightly odd because we are obsessed with knowing 'how our bodies work' and how we can make them work even better. We want, apparently, to see *bodies* as machinery, but brains (obviously bodily organs), or at least minds, as something somehow 'magical'.

This makes it hard for neuroscientists, and people working on artificial intelligence, to get a word in edgeways. Not surprisingly, they become deeply defensive (and therefore offensive). And, again not surprisingly, we do not seem to make much progress in what ought to be a fascinating and important area of science.

The problem is that we know now a good deal about how brains work: about brain cells, and synapses (that allow the cells to communicate with each other), and specialized functions (just as different bits of the rest of our body do specific jobs, so do different bits of our brains). We know a good deal, though not enough, about the complex relationship between hormones generated in various glands elsewhere in the body and their effects on the brain. We are learning more and more about how the different functions of the brain relate to each other (neural networks/bi-hemispheric studies) and how certain sorts of damage (strokes, head injuries, surgical intervention) can affect performance. We are beginning to learn about genes and genetic groups or clusters, and the ways in which they too can structure both intelligence and mental health.

The trouble is that all this knowledge does not quite add up to our own experience of *ourselves*.

In many fields of knowledge 'explanations' work. They allow our experiences to sit within a framework that feels secure; a mixture plausible enough and comprehensible enough. For example, the idea that the earth revolves around the sun is a 'good' explanation. It is predictive: it gives me solid grounds for hoping that the sun will rise tomorrow, and it frees me from ritual or ethical obligations – and moral fears – that I must somehow take responsibility for this by being 'good'. It covers the observable facts better than the previous explanations. It is useful; for example, it simplifies navigation and therefore travel.

As we learn more about our own biology we find that some explanations are useful in this sense. The circulation of the blood, for instance, both feels like a sensible notion and enables me to deal with arterial bleeding in a more hopeful and constructive manner. A better understanding of the reproductive system is likewise a useful explanation. I do not bleed on a monthly basis because I am naturally impure, nor because God hates women, nor to remind me that I cannot be an educated person even if I want to be. I bleed as part of an immensely complicated, delicate, and surprisingly stable system, which not only enables me to get pregnant, but also enables me to enjoy heterosexual sex without getting pregnant.

Explanations that work can be seen as stories that are 'good enough'. They satisfy real needs in useful ways. Their ability to satisfy depends partly, but not entirely, on how well they deal with known facts or observable results. Change the facts and we very much hope (since we go on trying to be rational) that we will have to change the story. A good example of this is the way European society used to believe that children belonged to their fathers. This was partly because they believed that the mothers already belonged to the fathers. But it was also because their biological story told them that the whole, complete – though tiny – human being was contained in the male sperm and that all that women added through pregnancy was 'nurture'. The discovery of the ovum, and of women's role in reproduction, changed the story. Nowadays, for this and a number of other reasons, children are seen to 'belong' primarily to the mother. I hope we will eventually have a story in which children belong to themselves.

But none of the stories about minds and brains and personality and me-ness are 'good enough' in this sense. The old story – of God popping in a little soul – has been undermined by radical new information. The 'it's all neural networks' story (or other similar stories) does not seem to be finding much resonance in a society that has, for at least two hundred years, been terrified of Frankenstein's 'monster'.

It is here that people who believe in God ought to be able to be useful. We ought to be disinvested. We have nothing to lose.

Perhaps we have a God capable of allowing the random

arrangements of electrical charges and organic cells, shaped by random mutations of their DNA, sloshing about in a pool of chemicals, to be so sophisticated that we cannot believe that they work that well.

Perhaps we have a God who, in the face of all the apparent evidence, is capable of managing dualistic 'soul insertion', despite appearing to have ruled out that option by committing himself – and us – to the processes of time and matter.

Perhaps neither of these stories yet allows us to determine the full plot – and we are still missing some crucial data, which will allow us to combine the stories, or establish a new one.

Any, all, or a combination of these possibilities present to us a God who is generous, intelligent, complex, patient, and abundantly creative. Any, all, or a combination of these possibilities offers us the opportunity to learn about that God, to rejoice and to live with eager excitement in the world that we are part of.

None of these possibilities can possibly 'diminish' God. Whatever else we may know or believe, we must know that a God who can be 'injured' by the speculations of some of the finest brains of our (rather brief) times is simply not a God worth bothering about. You can almost hear the angels sniggering at such a ridiculous notion.

Yet the fact is that Western Christianity, though often quite progressive on poverty and development issues, is remarkably reactionary (traditionalist) on scientific issues, especially those about identity. The problem seems to be *our* (not God's) mixture of arrogance and fear.

Whenever you hear anyone suggest that God is 'threatened' by anything, then you can be quite certain that what the speaker means is that he personally feels threatened.[7] No contemporary theory of 'mind' is suggesting that consciousness is not a reality. So why should we feel threatened if it turns out that we have consciousness because of a rational (if random) process rather than a non-rational (but stable) one?

It seems to me that although there are no reasons why we need to feel threatened, there are at least three reasons why we *do* feel threatened.

The first reason is simple. The mechanical-evolutionary explanation of consciousness does not *feel* like a 'good enough story' because it is *not* a good enough story. Those scientists who offer it are demanding that we take too much on trust: that we entirely override our response to Shelley's story – her fears, her doubts, and our own demonstrated inefficiency (to put it mildly) at using our advances in scientific knowledge in beneficial ways.[8] I have to say that the virulence of some of the supporters of this explanation does not help their cause by the hectoring and intolerant language they use. Professor Dawkins, telling me on the radio that anyone who continues to believe in God is 'intellectually lazy', makes his argument less, not more, persuasive (since it is demonstrably untrue). We do not have to accept everything the scientists tell us: they have been wrong before. Nor, although they too have been wrong before, do we have to despise anything our instincts tell us. I do not believe our instincts for a 'good enough story' are in very good shape at the moment: we have seriously undermined our ability to use myth and story constructively. But that does not mean that those instincts are completely useless either. The 'yuck factor' should not be ignored:[9] it should be noticed and tested. On encountering an idea that feels deeply counter-intuitive we need to ask ourselves, 'Why?' Why do I not like this idea? Why am I being offered it? Why do its proponents believe it? Why is it better/worse than what I think at the moment? We are not obliged to accept it – only to think about it.

The second reason is a bit more complicated. As human beings, we have a very high investment in our own uniqueness. We want to live on the planet, but we still want to see ourselves as not quite being the same as everything else that lives on the planet. All small children want to be noticed, as separate and different from everyone else, even if they have to behave very badly to get that attention. In many situations adults do not seem to have grown out of this (no doubt evolutionarily useful) behaviour. A great deal of endeavour has gone into working out exactly how and why human beings are different from other species, even our closest relatives. Tool-using, joke-making, bi-pedalism, face-to-face sex, non-reproductive sex, having pendulous breasts, prominent noses, bigger brains and, above all, language. Inch by inch biologists, sociologists, geneticists, and zoologists have nibbled into all these 'behaviours' and shown that in one form or another they are shared by primates or marine mammals or some other species (elephants may even have mourning rituals). This desire to be 'special' is being forced into a corner. So, if nothing else, we will continue to insist that we get our 'special' consciousness by some special route. For this reason we want to reject the idea that there is no real difference between brains and minds; that what we experience as things of the mind are really just brain activities of a highly developed kind.

It is time to grow up. I do not need to be unique to be beloved, to be happy, to be *here* – here, now, thinking, feeling, being. Just as a mouse has a tail and I do not, so I have an articulating consciousness and the mouse (so I believe) does not. It is a species difference; that's all. It probably has an evolutionary 'edge' for me – though presumably not for the mouse, which is managing very well without it. To be honest, I do want to be special: and I want my species to be special – I find it very difficult to give up the idea that somehow God has 'chosen us' (in preference to mice for instance). But I do not defend God in defending my own egotism.

I have a third reason why the mechanistic explanation of consciousness is not feeling like 'a good enough story', although I have no way of knowing whether it is right or wrong. It is about bodies. It feels to me as though we are being offered two contradictory descriptions of our mind's relationship with our bodies simultaneously. The issue is hard enough to get our heads around: to work out how we think and feel about ourselves. It is therefore particularly difficult that the physical sciences are not speaking with one voice.

On the one hand, the brain scientists are telling us that 'intelligence' is about mental processes (brain activities). The standard test for whether or not a 'machine' (something that is engineered by human beings) can be regarded as 'thinking' (like a human being) is called the Turing Test.[10] In this test a human is placed in one room, and invisible to them, but in communication via an

> Geese on migration fly in a well-known 'V' formation.
>
> There is nothing aesthetic about this – it increases the collective aerodynamism to a remarkable degree. Some commentators believe that the technique adds to the distance they can cover by over 40 per cent. The shape of the V creates a slipstream sufficiently powerful to conserve their energy to that extent. Of course, this imposes a great strain on the lead goose. Every couple of hours, high above the icy oceans, they have a change of shift; a new goose comes to the front of the V, and takes over. The exhausted goose drops back, and the whole flock, without losing a wing beat, readjusts so that the previous leader can fly in the best protected position in the whole V.
>
> We do not know how the led geese select their leaders.
>
> If a goose flies over Whitby, in Yorkshire, it will immediately drop out of the sky – dead. Long ago, some ancestor goose, mid-migration, stopped and stole grain from St Hilda's farm. She sent it on its way with a stern threat that this is what would happen if it, or any of its descendants, ever came back. Have you never seen skeins of geese dividing, splitting apart, to east and west, as they bash their way up the cold coast towards their nesting grounds in the Arctic Circle? Haven't you seen them regrouping on the beach just north of the racecourse at Redcar?
>
> Which of these stories sounds more likely, or, even, less unlikely?

electronic screen, is an artificial intelligence machine and another human being. The tester questions or converses with both the subjects of the test in any way she likes – including nonsense questions, gossip, information, computing activities, jokes. If a tester consistently cannot distinguish between the machine and the physical human being, the machine should be judged to have 'passed its Turing Test' and considered to be 'thinking'.[11]

On the other hand, socio-biologists and geneticists are urging us to see ourselves as living more in bodies than in pure mind; as more closely related to our animal relatives than we have been wont to think. They argue that much of our behaviour is not 'learned' in the mind, but imprinted on the body.

For example, a Turing tester could ask the computer if it were ticklish: the computer might laugh, even giggle, and say 'yes'. But a recent book[12] has suggested that we laugh *because we are ticklish* – it is part of the grooming behaviour that we share with primates. We laugh rather differently from chimpanzees because being fully bi-pedal has moved us towards the voluntary control of exhalation (breathing out). We have extended laughter from a physical response to a more abstract mental one, but essentially it is an animal behaviour, not an intellectual one.

Now the best roboticists are as aware of this as I am. They would say, rightly, that such responses – along with all the other things that humans learn through their bodies and from their senses – are none the less processed in the brain. Whether they are 'hard' or 'soft' wired initially, they are still replicable. Indeed that the ability to learn from the environment, to develop and alter behaviour and ideas in relation to external stimulus, is the interesting bit. Eventually, many of them are convinced, understanding the brain's circuitry will allow us to make robots who can start reproducing and evolving.

However, that is not quite the point I am trying to make. I feel that we are being given two different scientific stories about 'who I am', and that we cannot really cope with both at once. Bodies do matter. No religion has ever tried to argue that they don't. We get mixed messages from scientists (it's all in the mind; it's all in the genes) and mixed messages from philosophers and theologians (the soul is unchangeable and immortal; your body needs firm management). It is not altogether surprising that none of these add up culturally to a shared and consistent story of the self.

But the failure of the story, or the interpretation of what is going on, is not a reason to be afraid of finding out. For one thing we tend to find what we are looking for – researchers did not find a 'gay gene' just by happenstance; they were looking for it. They did not find a homophobic gene because they were not looking for it, though actually that would be much more useful.

Fundamentally, anything we find out at this point is going to reflect well on God's 'intelligence'.

These sorts of questions need to be seen as a positive challenge. We need to think out and explain what Christians really mean when we describe a person as a soul somehow stuck into a body; and as uniquely different from all other known life forms.

Evolution

> You are God. You want to make a forest, something to hold soil, lock up solar energy and give off oxygen. Wouldn't it be simpler just to rough in a slab of chemicals, a green acre of goo? . . . In other words even at the perfectly ordinary and clearly visible level creation carries on with an intricacy unfathomable and apparently uncalled for. The first ping into being of the first hydrogen atom *ex nihilo* was so unthinkable, so violently radical, that surely it should have been enough, more than enough. But look what happens. You open the door and all heaven and hell breaks loose. And evolution is of course the vehicle of intricacy . . . This is the truth of the pervading intricacy of the world's detail:

> the creation is not a study, a roughed in sketch; it is supremely, meticulously created; created abundantly, extravagantly and in fine . . . Look at practically anything – the coot's feet, the mantis' face, a banana, the human ear – and see that not only did the creator create everything, but that he is apt to create *anything*. He'll stop at nothing. There is no one standing over evolution with a blue pencil to say, 'Now, that one there is absolutely ridiculous and I won't have it.' If the creator makes it, it gets a stet. Is our taste so much better than the creator's? The creator creates. Does he stoop, does he save, succour, prevail? Maybe. But he creates. He creates everything and anything.[13]

There is a curious cultural phenomenon around at the moment. Theologians and physicists can respectably engage with one another. Intellectually you are allowed (just) to believe what the cosmologists tell us *and* argue the existence of God from that evidence. However, it is somehow supposed that if you believe in Darwinian evolution (evolution through random mutation and the survival of the fittest) you can't possibly also believe in God. There is also an implicit add-on clause, which goes something like, 'If you don't believe in Darwinian evolution you are stupid, and therefore if you believe in God you are stupid' (or mad, or neurotic, or simply bloody minded).

Of course, this is nonsense. Take four of the major players in nineteenth-century evolutionary thinking:

> Wilberforce did not believe in either evolution or extinction.
> Owen believed in extinction but not evolution.
> Lamarck believed in evolution but not extinction.
> Darwin believed in evolution and extinction.[14]
> All four of them believed in God.

No one can think of any of these individuals as intellectually lazy, or unwilling to apply their intelligence across a far wider range of interests and studies than most twenty-first-century scholars can even imagine. Interestingly, in the nineteenth century, it was more likely to be the poets[15] rather than the scientists who did not believe in God.

Darwin's *Origin of Species* was published in 1859. The first edition sold out before the publication date: this is very unusual for a serious, radical scientific book presenting a brand-new idea, which has profound philosophical and moral implications, although the author chose to play these down.[16]

It is difficult for us to realize how much excitement there was about Darwin's ideas. We tend to get the impression that he invented 'evolution', came up with the idea from nowhere, as it were. But by the late 1850s evolution was not a novel concept. For several decades before the *Origin of Species* was published, there had been a growing interest in fossil bones, archaeology, pre-history, geology. In addition, new biblical scholarship and anthropological understandings of 'cult' and 'myth' were leading many people to realize that the Genesis account of the creation was not a scientific thesis. People were beginning to grasp that species had existed which no longer existed, and that existing species had changed.

What Darwin offered was the first genuinely functional account of how this might happen. It was based on a series of wonderfully accurate observations.[17] By a solidly empirical method he demonstrated that evolution was *random*. Tiny variations crept into species all the time by *chance*. A few of them proved useful – and, in conditions that were changing, some of them proved vital. The individuals within the species that had this edge were able to produce more offspring than those that did not, so in the next generation there were both more individuals carrying the modification and more chance of it being emphasized or exaggerated. The best adapted would probably flourish, eventually to the extermination of the less well adapted.[18] In the next century the discovery of DNA and the double helix showed that there was something to mutate. (A mechanism for Darwin's mechanism consolidated the theory.)

The bit of Darwin that most people objected to was not really the idea that human beings were descended from monkeys, but that they were descended from monkeys by *chance*. The objection was exactly the same as Einstein's objection to quantum theory – 'God doesn't throw dice'.

This is a deep instinct: most people feel it. The discovery of how chancy, risky, and random the whole business really is, is often given as a reason for not believing in God. At the same time, many people who want to believe in God, like Einstein and the Victorian critics of Darwin, say to the scientists, 'It can't be like that, you just haven't done your job properly. There has to be a purpose.' God, we declare,[19] does not design a universe, or a species (especially the most important species of all – *me*) just by chance, by the flick of a wrist, a dice throw, randomly.

Why not?

We all know that the best creative moments are those when we let go of control and invite chance, the subconscious, the not-yet-realized, the beyond-technique, the genuinely experimental, into the work. This is not just true for art. It is true for prayer, for giving good parties, for educating young people, and for coming up with new scientific paradigms. We all know, as teachers or as students, that the best lessons, the most exciting and deep learning experiences, come when the teacher is able to let go, and allow the chancy expressions and questions of the pupils, let the random interactions and unplanned ideas develop. We all know too that this can equally prove a recipe for chaos. That is the risk; you have to chance it. Why should God's creativity be so utterly different from mine – since I got mine from God?[20]

In the second place, we really do know now that random events play a major part in creating the universe. Since we are part of the universe, shouldn't we expect random events to play a part in creating us?

In the third place, a God who creates randomly rather than *for* some useful end is a nicer God. If we want to have a God of love we might as well take a look at what we think love is. We certainly don't experience love as a thuggish bully standing over us, forcing us to do or be this, that, or the other. Can a God of love also be a highly efficient bureaucrat with a Five Year Plan (or Five Million Year Plan or whatever) in which every detail is perfectly thought out, immaculately planned, and nothing happens that isn't under the management of head office? Those of us who have the privilege of loving or being loved know that you do *not* gaze into the eyes of the beloved other with tenderness and passion and think, 'What are you for?' No. You think 'Wow!' or 'How come I'm so lucky'. Is God's love less generous than my shadowed version of it?

The fundamental point is that it *is* random. God does throw dice; does take chances, not just within the laws of mathematics, and the laws of sub-atomic particles, but here. Here within me. This is how it is. Galaxies have crashed and died; and out of their deaths are made the six tiny ossicle bones of my ears. Several whole forests fell over – crash – into damp peat and were petrified, and now there is unemployment in the North East of England. We did not need evolution through random mutation to demonstrate the energy, the abundance, the wildness, of God; but we may be able to use the central randomness of our own existence to learn that we are not that special. We are special actually, but we are special because (through random evolution) we have the opportunity to be conscious of all these facts.

This fact of random evolution seriously undermines the idea of a self, as an individual being, a pure spark of eternal fire wrapped up in a body. We are more deeply bound into a process than that. Rowan Williams has written, 'The self *is* – one might say – the past acting now.'[21] He is talking here about people's own stories, their autobiographies, but it is just as true at the vast evolutionary scale as well. Part of my past and my present is a little single-celled organism that split or failed to split. Not because some malevolent deity thought, 'I'll sacrifice a couple of million species, which I have made myself, so that I can have those human being things in about 300,000,000 years', but because it split or failed to split.

On the whole, Darwinian evolution (with a few time-scale modifications) is accepted as being a true description. But as a society we are acting very like the Church acted towards Galileo – we want to say 'yes, it evolves', and still cling on to the sense that we are free individuals, autonomous and independent, with 'rights' and self-direction.

We can't have it both ways.

At what point in this extraordinary and exciting story do we want to imagine that God 'decided' that the original plan, the generosity of random chance and creativity, needed a radical up-date? When, exactly, did God decide to go platonic on the universe and tuck in a new bit, the soul? If the traditional teaching of the Christian Church is right, then we are each ensouled (given a soul) at the moment of our conception. When were we conceived. Does each hydrogen atom have a soul? Each dead galaxy? Or does it begin with 'organic' forms?[22]

These are silly questions. Why are we so greedy? Why is it not enough for us to be a part of this 'miraculous' story, a part that can explore and articulate and rejoice in the story, and can conceive of a God who is capable of having it happen?

Evolution – and within it biological inheritance, genetic make-up – provides an arbitrary limitation on my 'freedom', on my individuality. Evolution binds us together, and binds us to our past. I am who I am because of the ecological and other circumstances that randomly happened to be going on, not just at one magical moment called 'creation', but over and over again throughout the period that there has been organic life on this planet.

We are not just talking about the colour of our eyes or the length of our legs. There is a close connection between physical characteristics and the development of character traits. I don't mean here just those characteristics that may be genetically inherited themselves. We are rapidly becoming aware that the sorts of bodies we have affect the ways we develop.

> Sometimes things are simply complicated. Not just scientific, technical or philosophical things. Life is complex, baffling and designed to keep us on our toes.
>
> Take, for instance, the case of Joan of Arc (1412–31). I'm not thinking just now of a 'diagnosis' or 'explanation' of her somewhat unexpected life; or of the cruelty and base disloyalty that the noble gentlemen of her time offered this courageous young woman; but of what has happened to her since she died.
>
> She was condemned to death as a heretic by a church (rather than a civil) court. Quite specifically, that court declared that in saying she heard the voices of St Catherine and St Margaret, 'she lied and was in error'. Twenty-five years later (in 1456), that verdict was quashed and she was declared innocent. Nearly 600 years later, in 1920, she was canonized. This means, of course, that the church was now satisfied that she had indeed heard the voices of St Catherine and St Margaret.
>
> In 1969, however, the 'universal calendar' of the saints was revised. A good deal of doubt was cast on the historicity of a number of early Christian saints; but only four saints who had had worldwide recognition had their cults formally and completely suppressed – they had not existed and should not be honoured. Among these four were St Catherine of Alexandria and St Margaret of Antioch.

At its very simplest: my dad fancied my mum; and, by a bit of luck, my mum fancied my dad. They had evolved bodies that let this happen, but did not oblige it to. They had both survived the war. Because of the way he had been brought up, because of his genetic inheritance, or because of good luck, my older brother (less than two at the time) did not scream in a manner that came between them fancying each other. That night. That couple. That ovum.

That particular sperm in 3 million. That set of chances. Me. And the same chancy business, over and over again, more times, more places, more blind luck than we can imagine. The human person, we are learning reluctantly, simply does not exist outside the billennia-old instabilities of the double helix.

Any God you believe in has to be a God who wants the world to be like that.

Psychoanalysis

So far we have looked at three fundamentally different stories about what it is to be a human being. Like all good stories, these come in slightly different versions, but basically we have:

1. The traditional model – inherited not from our Jewish roots, but from Greek classical philosophy. There are various refinements and details, but basically this story says that a human being is a spark of immortality, packaged in a body. The spark is spirit: immortal, eternal, and unchangeable. The body is matter: 'mean, nasty, brutish and short', but luckily not very important. On the whole, though for no particular reason, most people who believe this story absolutely believe that the 'spiritual' bit is vastly superior to the 'bodily' bit. In story terms, the body is the evil goblin who has captured the lovely princess and is keeping her (souls are curiously often female) imprisoned until the handsome prince turns up.
2. The animal model. A human being is a life form whose identity lies in the genetic inheritance of a million-odd years of random mutation, adaptation, survival, and reproduction (evolution). Our identity, our behaviour, our desires, and our social relationships grow out of that inheritance and are shared, to varying degrees, with other species. Our personalities, habits, gestures, and meanings are fixed by our specific genetic pattern.

On the whole, though for no particular reason, those who hold to the animal model tend to think that evolution is 'upwards' – things are getting 'better'.

3 The mechanical model. The story here is that there is not really a story at all: there is a poem and a riddle. The poem is rather beautiful, about criss-crossing power lines, webs, nets, tides, flows, and rhythms; it has a dense formal structure and some rich imagery. The riddle is about how a poem can describe and analyse itself. This is a poem with no poet. This makes us uncomfortable. On the whole, and perhaps for this reason, the people who prefer this story tend to insist that the individual person in it is not going anywhere – it is not a narrative or even an episode in a narrative: it just *is*.

It is hard to think of a nice liberal story, which lets all three of these tales work together in a co-operative style.

However, there is yet another story – another myth about 'what it is to be a person'. We tend to see it separately from these three stories and not always notice the conflict. This is the story of the self as told by psychoanalysis.

It tends to get separated from the others for several reasons.

One is that this story is a very new story. Freud published *The Interpretation of Dreams* in 1900: if Frankenstein was a nineteenth-century story about what it was to be a human being, then psychoanalysis is the big story of the twentieth century. It is so new, really, that it may still have development potential – just as Owen's (wrong) ideas about evolution allowed Darwin to develop his. Unlike the basic Darwinian story, or the basic Christian-philosophic story, it does not yet have a stable narrative. It isn't quite the right shape yet to be a myth.

Another reason is that the others are all classic 'myths of origin'. Myths of origin tell a group of people where it came from. They are very valuable stories because they unite people, bind them together as members of the group, and thus transform the group into a community. (They can also, of course, be a powerful way of excluding as well as including individuals.)

The psychoanalytic story does not look like a myth of origin. It looks like a 'hero' story – another very common sort of myth. It starts not with some grand creation-type beginning, but with a little baby. This baby is more or less a blank blob (although it turns out that it does in fact have some 'instincts') and it acquires a self through a quest; through a process.

None the less, it is a myth of origin: it purports to tell us how a human being comes to be a person, to 'own' a self. But it supposes, as only a twentieth-century story could, that we are not part of a community: we are individual, autonomous, and *the* central (perhaps the only) character of our own drama. It supposes that our births are the moment of origin. Thomas Aquinas argued years ago that each single angel was a separate species of angel. They were complete in themselves, and did not *need* each other (although might well enjoy each other), and consequently did not, for example, breed. The psychoanalytical story is a bit like that: other people become the sort of 'environment' that Darwin was talking about when he described adaptation. (There is another oddity about the psychoanalytical story: it tells us that, like the Judeo-Christian God, the individual creates itself by talking, by speaking (rather than by doing).)

In fact, Freud did precisely what Darwin did: he discovered a mechanism to explain an already recognized problem. Freud's problem was far older than Darwin's. Paul of Tarsus had articulated it very clearly in the first century AD: why is it that 'that which I would do I do not, and I do that which I would not'.

Psychoanalysis says, basically, that the person is forged in the act of living: the self grows and develops through experience, and through forgetting experience and converting experience into something else. A person is not a machine. A person is not a machine driven by a skilled engineer either. A person cannot (by means of reason, knowledge, or even self-interest) 'learn' to behave well. A soul cannot programme a body to 'be good', to 'act virtuously'. The movements of the subconscious are as real as acts of the conscious, the will.

As it happens, none of the three older stories are very keen on incorporating Freud's new story into their story. (All makers of myths of origin have to be a bit fundamentalist![23]) But Christianity has a particular problem. Christian theory (theology) has barely entered into any sort of relationship with psychoanalytic theory, although it uses – usually appallingly badly – psychotherapeutic techniques and jargon.

This is not surprising. There is a real sense in which psychoanalytic descriptions of the self 'downgrade' sin; 'upgrade' self-interest; reduce solidarity; and encourage autonomy and 'independence' while reducing freedom. Of course, if psychoanalysis is *true* or even helpful, we will need to get our heads around it; here I am simply looking at some of the reasons for the suspicion about it, and resistance to it, within much Christian anthropology.

The fact is that psychoanalysis, although it offers considerable illumination on aspects of the human condition, does undermine an old-fashioned view of sin. Christianity, however, needs sin. If there is no reality to sin, there is, in traditional language, no free will (and therefore no good acts either). More importantly, Christianity's most central claim is about redemption. We have been redeemed, bought back, by the generous self-giving and suffering of Jesus. If there is no real sin, then we don't need to be redeemed and the whole passion becomes a macabre joke perpetrated by a sadistic God. Redemption and forgiveness only make sense if sin is real. Many people in recent years have preferred to jettison Christianity rather than accept the reality of sin. But I believe that sin is real – mainly because I observe that I do sin. Sometimes I choose to do what is not in my interest as a member of a community, even though I recognize this and have alternatives.

To be honest, I feel out of line with most of my friends and acquaintances on this matter. They seem to experience a lot of guilt, but no sin. As this pointless guilt must be very uncomfortable, they are (sensibly) prepared to spend both time and money getting rid of it. But when I look at my own life I notice a good deal of sin and *not enough* guilt. Guilt is an emotional experience that alerts me to sin – or should do. Once I am aware of the sin, I have some chance of repenting of it and therefore being forgiven. The feeling of being forgiven is lovely. (It is so lovely that sometimes it is hard not to feel that the sin and nasty repentance are more or less 'worth it'. I am not defending this morally, I am simply observing a phenomenon.) But, anyway, quite apart from these feelings, I have an investment in the reality and seriousness of sin: the theological one I mentioned above, and a further sense that solidarity (co-responsibility) is more valuable to me than personal 'fulfilment', and that a belief in sin and forgiveness shifts the weight of human corporate life more heavily into the former camp.

Because of this investment I need to treat as a bit suspect the fact that I find sin more intellectually persuasive as an explanation of the horrendous mess I see within me and around me than the psychoanalytic story of individualism, autonomy, and repressed sexual urges. None the less, I am still left with a feeling that we have been rather overwhelmed by the Freudian story and need to sharpen our critical faculties.

Actually, there is more to it than this. Christianity, because of pride and fear, let itself be badly wounded by the scientific revolution. We really liked the geocentric universe, with ourselves at the centre – the universe's purpose and climax. In this universe, blessed directly by God, we could stand still, in our small still place, which had been designer-made for our convenience. The sun, the moon, and all the planets, all the great powers, were obliged to dance around us, for us; and the Church was in charge of it all.

'Wrong,' said Galileo, '*Eppur si muove*' [It bloody well moves].'

And eventually Galileo won, and the Church was forced to abandon hard-fought territory. Instead of praising God and moving forward in joy, Christianity came up with a brilliant defensive strategy: it privatized itself. It kept the old business, but 'downsized' radically. Now inside each *individual* was a small still place – perfect, eternal, immutable, designer-made, called 'the true self' or the 'soul'. Around it all the things of 'this world' – the pleasures of the senses, the challenges of learning, and politics and justice and 'virtue', all the activities of the body – danced for its edification. (Though rather less, alas, for its delight: astral bodies being less into sex than human bodies, they were rather more permitted to be delightful.)

Just when the Church had got used to its smaller kingdom (the Church moves slowly, 350 years is not very long), along comes Freud and pronounces the psychological equivalent of *Eppur si muove*. A self moves and changes and is shaped, pummelled, carved, formed by what happens to it. The child is father to the man. Identity is fluid, open to possibility, not fixed, not unchanging, and not entirely under anyone's control – not even its own.

In this context it is interesting to notice that the other theories of human personality that we began this chapter with (the biological and the mechanical) have as much difficulty with the psychoanalytical story as I do, though on rather different grounds. It fails as an explanation, because it is unprovable. It is not very predictive: you can't tell what sort of person you will get by moving even the known variables. And it is not very useful, because as a therapeutic tool (as an applied science) it does not seem to work; it does not deliver its stated results in any consistent or replicable way. Of course this does not make it 'untrue' or 'wrong', but it does rather question its status as a 'good enough story' to account for our abiding sense of self.

Evolution and genes. Brain function. Psychoanalysis. All these scientific disciplines in different ways challenge the human-centred traditional Christian notions that we are made up of two parts: a soul and a body. They radically undermine the notion that the soul is more real than the body. But they have not as yet provided a better or more satisfactory account.

As a scientific description, the Big Bang is 'better' than Genesis 1 and 2. As a scientific description, quantum theory is 'better' than a Newtonian 'divine clockmaker'. As almost any sort of description, Darwinian evolution is better than a God who runs around burying fossil bones within rocks in order to test our faith. But the new theories of mind and brain – although they make the traditional Christian dualistic explanation of the self probably untenable – do not seem sufficient to replace the older version in any immediate or straightforward way.[24]

Who am I? What is it to be *me*? What does it mean to say 'I am'? There is at the moment no certain answer. There will be. But, I repeat, all answers will be to the glory of God who made us this way, whatever way it is that we are made.

Psychiatry

One quite common way of learning what something is or how it functions is to look at what happens when things go wrong. The reverse is also true – and the relationship between, for example, human biology and medicine is intimate. The study of healthy organs helps doctors work out what is the matter with their patients and how to cure them; the study of pathology helps biologists understand normal functions better.

One might hope, then, that a quick glance at psychiatry – the medical speciality which looks at mental disorders and illness – might help us understand better what a well person *is* or might look like. Unfortunately, this sensible method does not work very well; culturally, we do not have a very accurate idea of what might constitute mental health. For a speciality that attracts so much money, so much media coverage, so much cultural attention and so many patients, psychiatry is stunningly bad at 'curing' anyone. So far, for the relatively minor mental disorders, no medical treatment has proven substantially more effective than time, and a friend to chat to. 'Post-traumatic stress disorder' is actually made worse (longer in duration; more severe in symptoms) by the energetic on-the-spot counselling now so fashionable.[25]

Meanwhile, the prognoses for the more serious mental illnesses are alarmingly poor. Despite lithium and other treatments, a hideously high proportion of individuals diagnosed with bi-polar disorder (manic depression) commit suicide. There are still no treatments for addictive disorders that prove successful with even half the patients concerned. The likelihood of people with schizophrenic diagnoses living satisfying lives, or being in full-time employment, is tragically low, even among those who are fully drug-compliant.

In the meantime, there is inadequate agreement about what symptoms indicate which mental diagnoses, or even who is mentally ill. Particular symptoms hop on and off the diagnostic lists. Homosexuality used to be a sign of mental illness; now it is not. Epilepsy used to be regarded as a sign of demonic possession, and later as a mental illness; nowadays, it is seen as a physical disorder. Hearing voices used to be treated as, at least potentially, a great blessing, now it is seen as a symptom of a serious psychosis.

To complicate the whole issue further, all societies have used mental illnesses as a way of handling dissent, non-co-operation, and unruly behaviours. With the possible exception of female reproductive medicine, no other clinical discipline has ever been used quite so widely as a form of social control.

In other branches of medicine, doctors may well disagree on treatment and even on precise diagnosis; but they very seldom get up in court under oath to argue about whether or not the patient is 'ill' at all. With mental illness this happens frequently. Meanwhile, individuals who believe they are ill are left homeless, and lacking basic support mechanisms. Other individuals who believe they are perfectly well are kept under lock and key, as though they were criminals (not *quite* as though they were criminals: criminals have fixed-length sentences and must have been found guilty of some offence before they are deprived of their liberty).

> In Mesopotamia, the land between the two rivers – the cradle of western civilization, that was old when the first Pharaohs stirred in their splendid graves by the Nile – they wrote in a script which is now called 'cuneiform': scratch and dash marks on mud that dried (they had a lot of mud that dried in Mesopotamia) and later chips and scratches in stone.
>
> In Mesopotamia, the land between the two rivers, they thought that birds were holy. Birds would come down the waterside and walk, hop and run in the soft mud. And when it dried, there for anyone to see, their feet, so light and fine and elegant, had left little markings that looked just like cuneiform. The birds, Mesopotamians understood, could speak the language of the gods and were spelling out the words of the gods. The birds knew the mind of the gods and tried to share it, in writing, in the drying mud. It was not the birds' fault that the people could not read it.

Despite such poor results and confused methodology, more and more people seek mental health treatment, apparently finding illness a 'good enough story' to account for their unhappiness or social difficulty or unsatisfactory lifestyles.

If we are culturally shaky on diagnosis and weak on treatment, we are almost totally clueless – or rather have far too many conflicting clues – on cause. Inherited genetic tendencies, chemical imbalances, social pressures, cultural forces (too much religion/lack of formal religion, for example, are both adduced as though they were 'obvious'), substance abuse, bad mothering (and sometimes even fathering), fish oil deficiency, childhood trauma, and alien abduction are all presented with complete conviction.

Professionally, individual practitioners tend to relate causes to available treatments. Psychotherapists go for childhood trauma and repression, because that is what 'talking cures' address. Prescribing clinical psychiatrists are likely (though it is not inevitable) to choose chemically based models, because that is their exclusive domain. And so on. However, patients, especially those whose illnesses are considered 'serious', are very unlikely to have much choice about who treats their case. And as none of these approaches can be demonstrated to work much better than any other, it is a bit difficult to determine which cause, or combination of causes, is most probable.

If the situation were not complex enough, there is a further distressing factor: mental illness (instability, lunacy, madness, emotionalism, behaviour outside the norm, non-rational excess, or deficient activity, etc.) tends to severely frighten 'well' people. Some physical illnesses do this as well of course, but not in quite the same way. This fear seems to lead to emotionalism and non-rational activity as quickly as mental illness itself does. So, for instance, medieval Northern Europeans somehow found it easier to believe that there was a vast wave of devil-inspired night-flying among otherwise socially marginalized and powerless women than to think of these women as in need of social and affectual support. It is nearly impossible to persuade contemporary Northern Europeans that the number of mentally ill people committing random and particularly hideous murders is not rising to epidemic proportions. In fact, all the evidence makes clear that the number of murders committed by diagnosed mental health service users is stable – and indeed declining – as a percentage of all murders.

Or, to take another contemporary example: many people want their children to have a clinical diagnosis of mental illness (usually attention deficit syndrome) and to be put on psychiatric drugs (usually Ritalin) because they cannot control their behaviour. But they want other people's children, whose behaviour cannot be controlled, to be treated as 'bad' rather than mentally ill. So the social messages we send out and the social controls we demand of our governments simply add to the general chaos.

In short, it is nearly impossible to look to psychiatry for guidance on the fundamental questions of what it is to be a healthy human being. However, it is possible to discern two conflicting ideas.

One idea sees 'autonomy' as central well-being. 'Well' people have boundaried selves; they construct and present themselves as individuals, who can distinguish correctly between what is inside and what is outside the self. Such people neither spill over into other people's lives, nor let others penetrate their boundaries. They are independent, self-contained, and fulfilled (filled full of self). Such a person may well be highly socialized and have good relations with other autonomous independent people, but they don't merge, slop, let themselves be taken over, or get confused. In fact, they are like a tiny version of the modern nation state: well governed internally and forming useful alliances externally. This tends to be the sort of person (crudely outlined here) that Freudian psychoanalysis seeks to develop.

The alternative way of seeing a mentally or psychologically healthy human being is exactly the opposite. Humanity is structured in social terms: to be 'well', a person should model this reality. Far from being autonomous, self-actualizing, or independent, people need to lose their isolation and merge into others. The looser their boundaries, the more they are open to and blended with the 'other', the more complete and healthy they are. It is worth remembering that Freud thought that religious belief was a neurosis in itself. In terms of his psychoanalytically 'well' person, he was right. People who believe in God, believe fundamentally in 'otherness'. They do not just believe that the 'Other' exists, they usually believe that it is more powerful and more important than they are, and that their well-being depends on letting it absorb them. For this to happen, they need to have highly permeable boundaries. The danger with such a model is that this sort of openness can leave individuals extremely vulnerable to exploitation, and to the darker aspects of the imagination. None the less, you will not be surprised to learn that I find this second idea both more convincing as a description of 'mental health', and more promising as a social model.

Unfortunately, there seems to be little room, at present, for negotiation between these two positions. Psychiatry has radically failed both its 'clients' – those deemed mentally ill – and society more widely as it looks for sustainable descriptions of selfhood and identity. This needs to be challenged.

The social sciences

My son, who is a zoologist, tends, like many 'hard' scientists, to laugh at what are commonly called 'the social sciences': subjects like sociology, psychology, anthropology, politics, economics, semiology, and psycholinguistics (to name but a few). He says they are 'pretend sciences' with 'sloppy, soppy methodologies' and are more like arts than sciences. Unfortunately, 'arts-side' intellectuals (often, sadly, including me) treat the poor old social sciences with a similar sort of contempt-in-reverse.

The fact, however, is that they cover a range of subjects that are of real importance and have great influence in our lives, and especially when looked at in relation to the sorts of sciences I have already been examining: cosmology, evolution, intelligence, and personhood issues. They do more than true 'philosophy', and a great deal more than contemporary 'theology' or 'ethics', to inform our daily lives about how things are, and therefore how they might be.

Their research methods may be rather different from those of the older sciences, and their results are too easily debased, but they are trying systematically and thoughtfully to look at what it is to be a person-in-community – rather than abstract, philosophize, moralize, prescribe, or dictate behaviour based on some idealized identity.

The important thing from the point of view of this book is that, by and large, they are finding much the same sorts of patterns and dynamics as we have been looking at in the 'hard' sciences. They add their weight to the picture that I have been drawing of the sort of created order we live in.

What Marxism, and feminism, and most studies of race, poverty, child psychology, communications, anthropology, criminology, sexuality, and peace/war teach (not with a single voice, but with multi-toned, variegated whispers and hints), is that human personhood is constructed in material circumstances.

For the eternal-soul-in-temporary-body theory to work, it is necessary to believe that the essential person cannot really be touched by temporal realities. To be eternal sparks of pure spirit, the souls need to be (like God) without 'qualities'.[26] But all the evidence we have suggests precisely the opposite.

To take a very basic example, most contemporary child psychologists who work in this field find that very young murderers have themselves been victims of abuse. They were not born 'evil'. This is not to say 'poor little things', but it is to suggest that we are all involved, and have all failed both the murderer and the murdered. Violence breeds violence; abuse constructs personalities and identities at a very deep level.

Likewise, as Marxist economics has shown, poverty and class are not just incidental circumstances – they do structure identity. Class is a consequence of the social realities of economics. Economics (what Marx called 'the base') actually creates culture (the 'super-structure') in the widest sense – including family life, social organization, child-rearing customs, ethical development, health, and health expectations.

In some ways, gender is the easiest example to look at. Oddly enough, quite a lot of people who believe in 'pure souls' manage also to believe that women are essentially and eternally different from men. This does seem to me to be unsustainable. I have no doubt at all that gender structures personality, through experience and social relationships. It may well also do so through infant psychology (because the girl child has a different relationship to its primary carer from a boy child – and will do so whichever gender the carer is) and through biology. But the difference cannot derive from the 'soul', because a soul is necessarily without any gender. (Gender needs a body; 'spirit' cannot be made of matter.) Feminism has not merely explored the ways in which women are socially constructed, it has also challenged dualistic notions of identity.

I believe that there is a gradual coherence of ideas within the social sciences. I do not mean by this that social scientists all agree with each other, either within or across disciplines. I mean only that the social sciences have become an important and popular field of study because most people do want to know more about what it is to be a human being. There is a growing sense that we must seek the answers precisely from those scientists who look at individuals, and the way they are being formed by social structures, within social communities. This approach to what is, after all, a properly important subject seems more likely to deliver answers than the abstractions of philosophy.

What might this mean in theological terms?

I believe it means that God has given us the most generous gift that an all-powerful God could possibly come up with. God has embraced, apparently joyfully, a 'reduction' in power in order to increase ours. God has invited us to be fellow workers – not servants, not employees, but colleagues, partners, members of the Board of Management. Whether we want to be or not, we are necessarily 'engaged in creating each other's humanity',[27] each other's personhood and identity.

If we want to go on believing in a creator God, then it has to be one who wants us to take responsibility for this. Relativism has been extensively criticized for blurring moral boundaries, but taken seriously it imposes a very high obligation to work for justice, to think intelligently, and involve ourselves consciously with the world. God has revealed in the fundamental nature of the universe and of human identity that we have no choice – not to act is to act. How we live will create the world in which we live, and in which future generations live. If I am mean or selfish it is not that I will go to hell (though I might), it is that the world will be meaner and more selfish than it need be. And God will consent to that. This is pretty scary. Freedom is always scary.

There is no way out. What it is to be a person is to be an individual-in-community. Not because that is morally better than isolation, but because it is simply not possible to be otherwise. There is no personality outside of community, and we work on (with or against) each other's humanity to have any of our own.

It is mutual. The child and the mother create each other. The child 'makes' the mother; you cannot be a mother without a child. You aren't a mother first, and then, with the qualification, so to speak, acquire a baby.[28] No one can be totally outside this cycle of co-creation: even people in comas, in PVS,[29] create (or at the very least co-create) their carers. You cannot be a carer without someone to care for.

Even a murderer needs another person: you cannot be a murderer without murdering *someone*. I am using this difficult example precisely to make clear that this is not a moral or idealistic point of view. The 'murderee' has no moral, causal, or personal responsibility for creating a murderer. It is just a fact; a 'how it is'.

The state of play

What I have been trying to show throughout this whole section is that at present it is impossible to see the world that our Creator God made as something absolute and stable. It cannot be an objective thing, brought into being by God's 'fiat', and continuing unchanged until God decides to bring the curtain down on some climactic last act.

Indeed, it is increasingly difficult to see the world as

planned – in the usual sense of having a pre-selected purpose – at all. In as much as it has a 'direction', it is the direction of 'time's arrow'. Time moves in only one direction (although at different speeds, depending on the strength of the gravitational field around it). But time is not passive like a railway track, a fixed course along which events run from past to future. Time itself is a force (like gravity) and a dimension. Time is an active part of new things happening. Causality, although powerful and effective, is not absolute. There is also chance – the random; the unexpected; the genuinely new whose cause was not, and is not.

Davies and Gribben expressed this in their book called *The Matter Myth*,[30] reminding their readers of a nineteenth-century defence of God, which insisted there was 'a ghost in the machine'. They wrote: 'There is no ghost in the machine, not because there is no ghost, but because there is no machine.'

There is no machine: no predicated, stable, mechanical, explicable universe.

There is also no viewing platform: no place where we can stand outside the show and watch it. We are the show – or, rather, we are part of the show. We are not visitors from another dimension, aliens, foreigners, sojourners, or refugees.

Instead there is a place of chance and risk. A universe in the continual process of remaking itself, randomly, but within some boundaries. New things happen: we cannot predict the outcome, not because we are too stupid, but because they are unpredictable. To be human, to be alive, is to participate in that instability and unpredictability; and to share in the responsibility for it. To be human, to be alive, is to be dependent on that process that we cannot control, and to be dependent on each other whom we have no right to control.

This is how it is.

And if this is how it is, then fairly obviously we do not have quite the sort of God that we liked to think we had.

We do not have a *Führer*, a dictator. We do not have a managing director. We do not have a nanny God, nor a gangland Godfather.

There are several possible responses to these facts. I shall look at four of them now:

1 The scientists are wrong.
2 God is dead.
3 God made it nice and stable and somebody wrecked it.
4 Wow!

The scientists are wrong

Certainly scientists have been wrong before. Although its history is rather less littered with schisms (long-term and deepening differences of order, method, and eventually culture), science has certainly had its heretics: its wide boys, its charlatans, its deviants, and its lunatics. But increasingly, throughout the last century, the sciences attracted more and more of the best brains, from a wider range of cultures and backgrounds than ever before. While they do not speak with one single voice on the details, there is a remarkable and growing consensus from all disciplines about the underlying realities. There may of course be more data to come in – the search for the Unified Field Theory (the 'Theory of Everything' as it is sometimes called) acknowledges this. Good scientists acknowledge this. But we can't count on it – the next batch of data might take us even further into the chaotic and random. We have to live *now* – we can't put it off until an uncertain future date. And right now, chance and inherent instability is the best description we have got.[31]

God is dead

This has been quite a popular response among liberal intellectuals. What we experience as post-modern human beings, they tell us, is a hideous sense of 'loss and mourning': God is dead and we roam a friendless universe, without family or roots. Not exiles, but orphans.

My first problem here is that I don't experience that – or anything like it. Of course, my experience is not proof of anything at all. Indeed, we now know very well that a failure to experience grief when it is appropriate (as in the death of people close to us) is a serious psychopathic symptom – 'denial'. But, then, all they are offering is their experience. So I feel entitled to ask: What have we lost? What are we supposed to be mourning?

We have lost an infantile passivity, which allowed us to believe, as healthy infants should be allowed to believe, that our Parent was sufficiently up to the job to keep us safe until we were older.

After the last earthquake in San Francisco, the seismologists went back to look at their records. They had recorded and recorded and still had been unable to give any useful warning; they were eager to learn. Their sensitive machines collect data day and night, and it was this they wanted to look at more closely.

There is, of course, constant seismological activity along the great fault on which the city is, perhaps foolishly, built. But they noticed something odd: a few moments before the main shock, there had been a tiny, different, tremulous, hard-to-spot shaking of the ground a few miles outside the city. It did not look like the usual deep grumblings that they were used to – but something on the surface, something quite new and unrecognizable.

They investigated. They found that the shiver emanated from an area of the countryside, which was farmed as orchards. A few moments before the major earthquake, three million apples had fallen simultaneously off the trees. Three million apples. And the sudden weight of their landing had shaken the surface enough to alert, to sensitize, the dials of the seismological machines.

We have lost any justification for splitting ourselves in half (into body and spirit) – a practice that has allowed us, directly and indirectly, to mess up the planet, possibly terminally.

We have lost the basis for a good deal of our arrogance and a lot of our mythology – both of which depended on a romantic notion of each individual as the hero of a short but highly dramatic comic strip.

And, those of us who were Christians while God was alive have also lost a mechanical saviour doll, who craftily dressed up as human, while keeping most of the privileges of the Godhead. This hybrid being was sent down from heaven to act out the role of a suffering servant and make us all feel very guilty. Those of us who felt guilty enough could then be rescued and taken back home like runaway schoolchildren whose attempts at freedom could be seen as rather 'silly'. As well as being rather tasteless, this whole business was also unnecessary since God was all-powerful and could have redeemed us without all this fuss.

These are certainly losses, but they do not seem to call for mourning, especially if you think about what we have gained.

We have gained companionship, *love*. Not as an emotion, but as a fact. We do not belong to each other in mutual concern because we are unselfish, generous, or good. We, that is all human beings throughout all human history in the universe we inhabit, belong to each other because we do not exist without each other. We create each other and are created by each other. 'My bones are the dust of the old red stars.'

We have at least gained adolescence,[32] and the hope of adulthood.[33] The world may look more scary, but also more exciting.

We have gained, for those of us who want it, a better expression of the mystery of the incarnation. Our not-aloneness takes on a new depth. If Jesus became human, we became incorporated totally, simply by the actuality of what it means to be a person. God is committed to the project.

We have gained a secure basis for self-respect. I don't

have to hate my body, because it is imprisoning my soul, or dragging me down to a 'lower level'. It is me. I don't exist without it – the flesh of it, the history, and the particularity of it. (This ties back into Christian ideas about the resurrection of the body. We can gain a realization that there can be no resurrection without the body because there is no body to resurrect.)

So I don't think that the facts of science as we understand them really call for the resignation, let alone the death, of God.

God made it nice and stable and somebody wrecked it

This response has a sneaky attraction to it. It is a re-play of the Garden of Eden, the Genesis story. God made the world and it was 'very good'. There was no death, no work, no violence, and the weather was always nice. 'Very good' includes causality, foreknowledge, and control by God. Human beings sinned and that destabilized everything. Not just human morality and will, but the very laws of physics themselves.[34] (You can have an add-on to this scenario: the incarnation rectified everything and the left-over evidence, appearance of things, like death, are but an illusion and have 'no dominion'.)

This is theoretically possible, a bit like the nineteenth-century anti-evolutionary argument that God had created the world in seven days but had planted the fossil record, either for our amusement or to test our faith. But it is tricky – because we now know that the cosmos *so much* predates this Fall. We would not want to argue that the stars sinned – which is why they were destabilized and exploded; because if that were the case, then Christ would have to come as a star, not a person.

But, more important than being intellectually tricky, such a way of viewing the universe would be a pity – because what we have got is so fabulous. While I can see stinging nettles and HIV as corruptions of God's original plan, I would find it impossible to see the world that contemporary science is describing as a corruption of anything – what could be *better*?

Wow!

It will not surprise any attentive reader if at this point I say that I consider an awed 'wow!' the proper response to the world that we have got.

Wow! God is even smarter than I thought.

Wow! This gives me a chance to think about a God more complex, more interesting, and more desirable than the older model.

Wow! Nothing in this threatens the narrative of my faith. The incarnation of Jesus, the nature of the Trinity, and my hopes of salvation are all deepened, enriched, and secured in this science. God's love – an adult, passionate, free, and generous love – is manifested in the atom and in the far-flung cosmic spaces beyond the reach of our telescopes; it is demonstrated in our bones, our brains, our blood cells, and our social connections with one another.

No, there is no safety, but there is a wild delight: a deep beauty, a continuous and reliable source of joy. Wow!

So What?

If this is a plausible description of the universe, as we currently understand it, then what can we say about the God who created it?

If this is how things really are, or even if this is the best we can do to describe them, then how ought we to act?

When we ask this sort of question we must always remember that there is a famous philosophical impasse: you cannot deduce an 'ought' from an 'is'. No decent science offers moral instruction – no good scientist suggests the Theory of Everything will be a theory of everything; what it will do at best is carry on the work that Einstein started when he unified matter and speed. It will not tell you whether it is right to dump your boyfriend, shoot Hitler, or believe in God.

Even the social sciences – although they are often highly moralistic – are supposed to be descriptive, not prescriptive. They can outline consequences, but they cannot tell you whether or not you ought to choose those consequences. Psychology, for instance, describes a certain level of self-esteem; and the ability to place personal limits on the demands and desires of others leads to better functioning and higher well-being. It does not show self-respect (of this sort), to suffer and die for someone else – yet we collectively recognize that some acts of ultimate self-sacrifice are none the less the right thing to do. Jesus did not need a short course of behavioural therapy to eliminate his doormat tendencies, and lack of self-esteem. This does not make the psychologists wrong (although I do actually think they are wrong here, because they have underestimated our bound-together-ness): it simply means that you cannot deduce an 'ought' from an 'is'.

The trouble is that almost all modern human beings prefer doing to being. It is very hard for us to sit and look at something (anything) without asking, 'What is it for?' Or, 'So what?' And what God is *for*, for far too many of us, is morals: 'good' behaviour; for telling us what to *do* and how to do it. (As a matter of sad fact, too many religious people, especially in the West, seem to think that what God is *for* is authorizing us to tell other people what to do and how to do it.) All too often we first assert the existence of a God who does not make sense in the light of what we see or learn around us; and then short-cut to a set of rules which this God is supposed to demonstrate.[1]

Apart from anything else, this does seem rather unfair on God. As far as the creation goes, God does not behave like a rule-maker. Take a look around you: the world is preposterous. The God who made it seems prepared to let evolution, time, and love generate almost anything.

What I have been trying to say through this book is that if we look at the creation, and ourselves within it, we can indeed see the thumb-prints or brushstrokes of God – but what a God! A huge wild God; a God of chance and risk; a God of almost unimaginable generosity.

God may well be omnipotent (all-powerful, all-mighty), but this power is exercised in a very unusual way – by letting other people and powers be responsible, by consenting to work with whatever comes to hand. By preferring, apparently, the odd and the beautiful to the orderly and the simple; the risky and the chaotic to the safe and the calm; the big to the small; the long view to the short. (This should not come as a total surprise as it seems rather close to Jesus' ideas about power (within the human and social scale) too.)

We have a God who is abundantly creative and extremely

intelligent. And at the same time profligate, careless, open-hearted and not in a hurry. A God who is prepared to watch galaxies burn themselves away; to allow black holes and quarks to play tricks on time; to have humans develop absolutely unique thumb-prints – one by one across several hundreds of millennia; one who lets the continents themselves crawl or drift clumsily across the planet.

Can we seriously believe that this God did all this just to inform us of who should be allowed to have sex with whom? And, if so, is this a God we can find any time for at all?

Actually, I do deeply believe in morality, in ethics, in the life-long struggle to behave well; to behave in my own best interests which are the interests of my fellow human beings and the world. Because I believe that I don't want to cheat or take short-cuts, or refuse to look the truth in its wide but indifferent eye. I think there are places we can properly consult to get some guidelines. (I would suggest that both the Scriptures, and the 2,000-year-long meditation on them that we call the Tradition, the teaching of the Churches, offered some pretty profound and helpful thoughts on the subject.) But we cannot lean on the data. We need the best, most accurate, most illuminating information we can get; and then we have to use it in responsible, honest ways.

The point, as I suggested at the beginning, is that God reveals the divine in various ways. They do not have to be identical, but they do have to be coherent and non-contradictory. We do not want to contrast the God of Justice with the God of Mercy; the God of Chaos with the God of Order; or – in this particular case – the God of Creation with the God of Law. It is difficult to understand how the whole thing can hold together. Fortunately, humans can understand and use things without fully comprehending all their parts or precisely how they function (in my own case, examples are the combustion engine, the video recorder, and my own sexual responses).

For all these reasons I am very hesitant to set up some little algebraic formula, which says God is X, therefore I (or you) must do Y. Instead of trying to draw down 'rules' or 'commands' based on this exploration, I want to try and look at 'responses'. What might be appropriate responses to what it seems that God might be revealing to us by letting the cosmos be the cosmos that it is? That cosmos includes us, and the ways we communicate with each other, and how it is to be able to say 'me', to say 'I' and 'thou', in the huge and weird universe that we are a part of.

Specifically I want to look at three responses that seem to me not so much moral as emotionally necessary and sensible:

1 A respect for creativity; for art.
2 A commitment to our own collective humanity. You can call this justice or love, but I prefer at this point simply 'commitment'. We are covenanted to each other, far beyond moral choice.
3 Joy.

And all of these I sincerely believe grow out of a still more primary response, which – provided we are not reduced to blind terror – must almost inevitably and spontaneously well up if we believe both in God and in what the scientists are telling us about matter and the universe. That response, as I described it at the end of the last chapter, is:

Wow!

The fancy name for this gob-smacked, punched-in-the-solar-plexus pleasure is 'awe', and its articulation is an intake of breath; a sub-verbal breach in the space between me and the world; an ejaculation of delight. Wow! From this, may or may not come gratitude. Awe is not gratitude. Gratitude may sometimes even be an evasion of awe. But I do not see how we can look at the whole business, whether or not we believe it has any purpose, any maker, or any destination, and not feel a little giddy with awe and delight and amazement.

Bones are heavy. The normal human head – bone and brain and muscle – weighs between 5 and 7 kg (12 and 15 lbs).

To make flying easier, birds have evolved light bones; hollowed out like honeycomb. Compare the weight on your hand of a sparrow and a mouse and you can see how much difference it makes. We don't know which came first – the light bones or the flight – and it does not matter. A dynamic relationship can start on either side; now a goldfinch can alight on a thistle head and eat the seeds and scarcely bend the stalk. Ravens can tumble head over heels in mid-air and loop the loop for the delight of their sexual partners.

Darwinian evolution can explain that, and lots of other things too. But not everything. Sometime around the age of 50, women's bones start to hollow out; in some cases they become honeycombed and fragile, not heavy like a mammal's, but light like a bird's. Sometimes, later, they even develop, between their shoulders, a high, tight dome. A hump or hunch we call it.

Lamarck, unlike Darwin, believed in evolution by desire, by aspiration. Suppose for a moment he was right in some cases. Or imagine it, dream it for a space. Are such menopausal women aspiring to wings, to flight? Do they desire to be birds? Or witches? Or angels?

Indeed, one of the more endearing things about Professor Dawkins' atheism is the sense you get that he hates religion because it undermines awe in the astonishing world he wants to describe. And too often he is right. The Christian determination not to be overwhelmed by the sheer materiality of the material world, to see it as no more than 'a snare and a delusion' (while also claiming that our God made it and manages it), is one of the most offensive stances of contemporary faith.

A respect for art

The first thing we know about God is that God creates.

In the beginning God created.

Before God redeemed, commanded, sanctified, punished, or blessed, God created.

God goes on creating in a continuous act of power.

All monotheist religions that I know of additionally believe that God created self-consciously, deliberately: not by mistake, or in passion, or accidentally. (There are religions that believe in all these and in innumerable other sorts of creation.) Certainly all the mythologies that come out of the near Middle East believe that God created *ex nihilo*, from nothing, because God willed – wanted and chose – to do so. We cannot honour that God and not at the same time honour the creative acts that are God's primary form of self-expression. If we are in some sense 'made in God's image', then we have to honour all our own creativity too. It is as near as we can get to 'being like God'.

This is perhaps a bit dishonest because before God created, God *loved*; and therefore loving is as near to 'being like God' as creating is. But we ourselves cannot love until after we are created.

Everyone is necessarily creative.

'To breathe in is to be inspired; to breathe out is to give thanks.'

Just by drawing air into our lungs (or even having it pumped into our lungs by a machine) and expelling it involves us in a fundamental creative act: we take something, process it, change it into something new, and give it back to the outside world. Just by existing, as I argued in the previous chapter, we create relationships; we create each other and ourselves.

To acknowledge this, however, is not to confuse it with the self-conscious, deliberate business of creating art. Artists create like God does (though probably not as well). If we want to understand more about this work of God's, then we should be paying art the most serious attention – we should be listening to artists and looking at/listening to/absorbing the things they make.

It is a long time since theology has done this.

Most anthropologists now believe that once upon a time

religion and art were the same thing. We do not know exactly why a group of cave dwellers decided to adorn their walls with pictures of animals and hunting, but we do know that the impulse was not 'interior décor': it was religious. Singing, dancing, drama, and poetry all emerged from religious ritual.

It has been a long time since this connection was recognized.

I believe that we have lost, or are at least in danger of losing, a profound human skill: the ability to participate as audience[2] in art: in representation, myth, story, or symbol. Or, more crudely, we are neglecting our ability to think more than one thought at a time; or to recognize that something can have more than one meaning at a time. Instead we argue about which meaning it 'ought to have'.

This is what fundamentalism – whether biblical, scientific, or some other kind – is about. It says that this is the way you must read the text. There is no other way. 'The Bible is literally true, it must be read like that; you can't also have a poetic, symbolic, cultural, or historical reading.' Or, 'The scientific method is the only method for telling the truth.' I strongly suspect that any European before the eighteenth century would think this was very 'primitive' or stupid of us. For them, almost everything was both an object to be named, looked at and – if appropriate – used, *and* a symbol of divine truth. Believing that a lamb represented Christ did not stop you eating it.

We now prefer 'role models' to patron saints. We need the role models to be 'just like us'. A more open society wanted 'role models' to be the opposite of themselves – for instance, in most pre-scientific societies the patron of women in labour was a virgin. Artemis/Diana for the classical world; Margaret of Antioch for the medieval Christian. At the symbolic level, this makes complete sense; to a more literal mind, it does not. That is a huge cultural difference. You see the same thing at work in the way we want the royal family to behave 'like ordinary people'. Why have a monarch, an undemocratic symbolic ruler, if he or she is going to be 'just like me'?

When we come to thinking about God this starts to matter very much, because we cannot speak about God in anything other than 'imaginative' language; all our names for God are only analogies. If we press any of them too far we end up in a whole lot of trouble. When we say God is a Father, for instance, we don't mean that God is male, has a penis, and impregnates women. Jesus cannot be both Lamb and Shepherd *at the same time*. But if we have no developed capacity for using myths and symbols, we too easily get into a dreadful tangle.

Comparing God to a father, Jesus to a baby sheep, the Church to a family, or the Creator to an artist, is probably getting it the wrong way round. The right way round is the reverse: a lamb may be compared to Jesus' sacrificial action; the family can model itself on the Church; biological fathers ought to behave more like God does. We need to extend ourselves from where we are towards the unlimited God, not reduce that God to the level of our limited personal experience.

When we look at the artistic, the poetic, and the complex way that God works in the creation, we need this sort of artful language to describe both what we see and our response to it. We need to develop some artistic muscle, and the best way to get it is by honouring artists, by honouring that form of creativity that comes nearest to one of the central ways we can see God.

We can honour artists by enjoying the art they make.

We can honour artists by trying to understand works of art we don't instinctively enjoy. I listened to a conversation recently in which the Damien Hirst pickled sheep was under attack. ('Call that art?!' and so forth.) One person was silent; she was finally asked what she thought and she said, 'I don't know, I haven't seen it.' There was a shocked moment of silence; because – it transpired – no one else had seen it either (including me). This was especially interesting because the conversation came out of another one about how 'they' could not understand or legislate for the countryside – because as 'townies' Westminster politicians had no real experience of it.

We can honour artists by honouring artistic endeavour in small children, and especially in schools. We want schools to deliver 'basic skills' and civilized behaviours. Creative ability ought to fit into both categories, but they are being squeezed out.

We can honour artists by having more respect for youth culture. When we are confronted by a young person who has spent hours of time and labour and energy creating a new thing out of base matter – out of her hair, out of carpet dye and scissors and a razor blade; who has changed boring safety pins into jewels; who has pricked out the equivalent of the Sistine Chapel ceiling indelibly and painfully on her skin; who has in short acted like God with the only matter available to her – her own flesh – how often do we say an awed 'Oh, Wow!' or thank her for acting in a tiny way 'like God'?

Last year I had an argument with my son. He wanted me to drive all the way to his university and collect him and his music decks. I said he could take the train and leave the decks behind. He said I would not say that if he played the cello. This was true and perceptive of him. He went on to say that electronic 'mixing' was as much a musical instrument as the cello. I tried to argue that with the cello you made your own music and with mixing you did not. He said that this was ridiculous on two counts. One, no one made their own cello, the musical fragments he used were the equivalent of the strings, bow, body frame, etc., and that the music from a cello was every bit as much preconstructed as a mix. Two, most cellists played other people's music anyway – there was not a lot of jamming with classical string instruments, but his mixes were new every time. In the end I went and fetched him, along with the music decks – not because I am entirely persuaded by his answers, but because I know I would have gone if he had played the cello, and that is not fair.

We are, of course, allowed to honour artists by disliking

some of the art; by distinguishing between 'good' and 'bad', and by having personal preferences as well. But they should be preferences not prejudices; and they should always be informed by the realization that you cannot get good art without allowing a good deal of bad art. Here, of course, the analogy breaks down – God does not need to practise to get perfect.

And in the end we honour artists by acknowledging and accepting and delighting in the fact that art is not for our edification and moral uplift. It is not for 'good community relations', nor to sort out problems, nor to make my theology easier for me. It does not have a moral imperative. Ultimately it is *for* joy, for complexity and mystery, and its own ends.

A commitment to one another

In the Big Bang, in the quantum sphere, in evolution, in history, and in all the ways that we become 'selves', God has made a radical and generous commitment to us as bodies (matter) and as communities (mutually dependent organic societies). I can find no evidence in the description of the universe by contemporary science – although it is discernible in other forms of God's revelation – that God has made any such commitment to us as individuals or as 'souls'.

If there is any content to this description, then our commitment to one another, and to the past, the present and the future, becomes, like God's, a commitment to our own nature. 'Alone with none but thee, my God, I journey on my way' is simply not a plausible statement. There is no 'I' in solitude of this kind.

To put it another way, in *Capital* Karl Marx believed that he had shifted socialism from a moral engagement to elevate the oppressed, into scientifically based self-interest. This is why Marxism has often described itself as 'scientific socialism' as opposed to 'utopian socialism' – the pre-Marxist optimistic egalitarianism of many nineteenth-century radicals, like Thomas Owen. The argument was that the science of economics demonstrated that capitalism *would* collapse. Not that it would be a good thing if it did collapse, or that the proletariat should work to make it collapse, but that such a collapse was inevitable and that this was demonstrable and evident. It would be followed, equally inevitably, by either the rule of the organized proletariat or by 'barbarism'. It was therefore in the enlightened self-interest not just of the workers to organize, but of the bourgeoisie to 'invest' in that development, and ultimately in the revolution itself. (As it happens, Marx was wrong. He underestimated, among other things, the ability of capitalism to shift from nationalist competition into a global, super-national, post-imperialist power.)

By analogy, I am suggesting here that our present understanding of the way the world is shifts us from a 'utopian' or moral commitment to one another – 'it would be good if we all took care of each other' – to a 'scientific morality', which implies that it is in our enlightened self-interest to do so. Not just because it is true, but also because we will not flourish if we do not.

This radical commitment, growing out of our awe at the universe that God has created, and at the sort of God we learn about from the universe, must express itself in a morality that is necessarily as political as it is personal. One of the saddest things that religion has done in the face of modern scientific thinking (and also, crucially, in the face of economic thinking) is privatize morality and spirituality. This is not the fault of the scientists, even those who are opposed to religion; it has been an odd withdrawal, a mixture of arrogance and fear, both by Christianity and most of the other faiths of northern Europe.[3]

We have reached a strange cultural place where an elected political leader can say, 'There is no such thing as society.'[4] Where pundits can seriously say, 'Religion should keep out of politics.' ('Religion should keep out of morality'?) Where the feminist slogan 'the personal is the political' is seen either as wildly revolutionary or as an excuse to evade political activity. These are radical misunderstandings of how things *are*.

By designing a highly risky cosmos, God has made a reckless gamble. By setting us free, by creating the universe in such a way that it participates in its own becoming, God has ruled out the 'cavalry option': a regiment of angels is not going to come galloping miraculously to our rescue. What we make is what we get. We need to face up to this: morality has a grim seriousness that we may have underestimated. (We should not have, incidentally, because as a matter of fact the modern scientific model only underlines what the Scriptures, particularly the Hebrew Scriptures, the 'Old Testament', had already told us.)

Near the beginning of this chapter I said that it was possible to call this commitment to our collective humanity 'justice or love'. I chose not to do so there because I wanted to underscore my understanding that there is no choice about this, but now I would like to reintroduce the terms, though stressing very strongly that they are short-hand for the larger inevitability of our union, and not optional personal choices. Another of the symptoms of the cultural situation we are in, another sign of how profoundly we are fragmented, is the fact that 'justice' and 'love' are now seen as somehow opposed to each other. Simone Weil, the French philosopher, describes 'justice' as the attempt to act towards people we were not able to know as though we 'loved' them. 'Love' for her was the intimate expression of 'justice' – and 'justice' was the long-distance expression of 'love'. The two were fundamentally one: they were two 'styles' of manifesting our Siamese-twin relationship to one another.

I could look at what this might mean in almost any area of life, but I am going to take sex as an example. I have picked it because of its connections with religious thought. Religion has made sex its particular and especial business. Indeed, the word 'morals' has come to mean little more than sexual practices. In fact, we have an obsession with sex; or, to be precise, with one rather minor aspect of sex – coitus.

There is a great deal of concern throughout the world both about reproductive technologies and about population levels. But one falls into the private sphere and the other is seen as political: neither is treated as a justice issue, and they are not treated as connected in any significant way at all.

The Cairo population conference in 1994 came to the conclusion that the anticipated rate of population increase throughout the world in the twenty-first century was dangerous – both to development in the traditional areas of poverty (the Third World) and to resources globally (it was everyone's problem). The agreement on this was probably as near as a genuinely international conference has ever got to unanimity. There was less unanimity about what to do about it (with the Vatican conspicuously, and several Islamic and some other African states also, strongly objecting to any formal linkage between aid and contraception supplies). But the conference did issue a clear statement that the increase in opportunities for women, both in terms of education and economic independence, was the most effective way to lower birth rates; and that aid projects should be directed towards this end. Moreover, the conference drew attention to the fact – perhaps a slightly surprising one – that lowering infant mortality rates, and thus increasing the number of children who survived, also reduced birth rates and eventually population sizes. A couple of years later the women's conference in Beijing came to almost identical conclusions.[5] Thus at the global, political level, population increases were being treated as a serious matter. Politically there was strong agreement that this was not simply a Third World problem, with which the developed nations might charitably help, but a problem affecting resources for everyone – with further implications for world peace.

Shortly after this it was discovered that European birth rates were falling. At about the same time it emerged that sperm counts in northern Europe were also falling and that consequently infertility was increasing (which would, of course, further lower birth rates). You might have thought that this was excellent news; it meant that Europe could make a fairly painless impact on a world problem. It vindicated feminism and the contested politicization of women's rights. It even gave men, without undue effort, a chance to make a contribution to a problem that they recognized – but realized would have to be made mainly by women. You would be wrong: the figures were widely reported in the various news media and were seen almost entirely negatively, as bad news rather than good. It was treated as a personal and moral issue rather than politically. Feminism had produced 'selfish' women who were not prepared to bring up children. Family life was threatened. Sexual continence was undermined. Children would be over-indulged. And so on.

Meanwhile, over the last decade the British government has not substantially increased international aid.[6] However, it has used its 'buying power' to take qualified education and health staff out of developing countries for our own use, and has massively increased funding for fertility treatment.[7] This 'right' to have a child stands in an odd relationship to our social dislike of other people's children and the fact that we, as a society, are seriously failing the ones we have got.[8]

'Sex' is not just a matter of private love or personal sin, despite our current obsession with it. Who is doing what, and with what and to whom, is not just a matter for psychotherapists; it is matter for human society, it will shape our future, because of some blind chance mutation in an organism in the primal goo. We are our brothers' keepers; and every human being is our brother.

But so indeed is every atom. 'My bones are the dust of the old red stars.'

Morality – or how we live best in the world we have got – is not just a private or individual matter. This larger scale of thought, to match the huge scale at which God works in the creation, can obviously be applied to more areas than just sex. God has agreed to 'go along with' both nature and culture. This expanded vision of ourselves, our identities, and our place in the cosmos, can most obviously be applied to issues like ecology and conservation, global poverty and debt, and the sorts of science and scientific experimentation we should work towards funding and succouring. But it also applies at the intimate, so-called 'private' level. If the reality and growth of my self (or your self) lies not in my own autonomy, but in my dependence, not in my 'fulfilment' but in my open-heartedness, then even my praying and my loving need to be restructured in the light of this information. (We would swiftly move our financial investments if we discovered that the fund they were in was based on untrue and out-of-date information.)

Joy

In the Gospels Jesus offers very few direct explanations as to what the incarnation is *for*. The Gospels are not functionalist or pragmatic texts. On the whole, the way the gospel is presented rather overlooks this – we are told over and over again rather precisely why Jesus became human: 'he died that we might be forgiven, he died to make us good, he died that we might go to heaven' and so on. (And I think there is a clear *narrative* thrust (story line) that suggests that many of these motives were important to his sense of mission or to the Gospel writers' understanding of it.)

But one of the few truly functionalist explanations that Jesus did offer directly for his incarnation and forthcoming death was: 'that my joy may be in you and your joy may be full'.

It is in the knowledge – gleaned here and elsewhere – that God desires our *joy* that we should look at the creation we have been offered. I have suggested throughout the book that the new sciences of creation give us the strongest possible ground for joy; and that the people who see nothing but 'loss and mourning' in the new universe we inhabit are mistaken.

Now at the end of this book I want to go further: I want to suggest that 'joy' is our duty. Joy is the correct moral response to a clear-eyed look at the world we find

Abraham has always seemed a rather dodgy role model to me. Among his many unattractive activities, he gets extremely rich off his wife's immoral earnings (Genesis 12.10–16); and he is willing to kill his supposedly beloved son to please his boss and gain material advantages (Genesis 20). He is almost certainly insane and demonstratively selfish, autocratic, lecherous, cowardly and violent. Sarah is not a lot better – she sends Hagar and Hagar's small child out into the desert to die, apparently because of a 'contemptuous look'.

But...but they laugh.

They laugh with God, they even laugh at God. There is not a great deal of laughter in the Bible, but when God proposes yet another of his rather long-term covenants – this time involving circumcision (and more promises of a baby for the now elderly Sarah) – Abraham laughs so hard that he falls flat on his face. Sarah (perhaps rather better mannered) tries and fails to suppress her laughter, smothering her giggles in the tent flap. El Shaddai, the Almighty, who brought them up from Ur through the desert, chivvied them out of Haran and south into Canaan, famine-drove them into Egypt and summoned back again, goes on making preposterous offers and they go on laughing. Laughing and obeying.

And finally, at last, they get the baby. Are they humbled, awe-struck, grovelling, solemn? No, not at all. 'Isaac', they call the baby. 'Isaac, God's laughter'. God laughs with them. They laugh with God. They are blessed beyond the reasonable.

ourselves in. This seems odd to many people; and indeed it seems a bit odd to me too. But I think this is because we have not properly understood what joy is.

The word 'joy' is closely linked to two other words: the French verb *jouer* (to play) and '*jewel*'.

Joy is play, playfulness, a game. Games work best (everyone has most fun) when all the players recognize that although the rules are arbitrary, contingent, and could be different, for the duration of this game they will all accept them. If we believe, as I have argued that we must believe, that the universe is constructed by chance, by random events functioning within deep laws, then it is right to see it all as a game; and thus all as a joy.

Joy is the treasure buried in the field, the pearl of great price. In the biblical parable, once the merchant knows about the jewel, he simply sells all that he has to purchase it. This is not a parable about the cost of discipleship: it is exactly the reverse. Once you have identified such a treasure, getting hold of it is entirely obvious; no more than a sound investment. The problem is only in finding a reliable 'jewel detector'.

The traditional detector offered by Christian experts is gratitude, thanksgiving. And there is nothing wrong with good manners. However, it is a little hard to be convinced that the sort of risky, gambling God, the huge wild God that we seem to have, is primarily interested in good manners. Moreover, as we are all too horribly aware, 'gratitude' is not a very good basis for a relationship. The most poisoned form of this obligatory gratitude is parents expecting their children to behave in arbitrarily set ways and then be *grateful* – 'because of everything I have done for you'. How many teenagers have fled from how many rooms shrieking that they never asked to be born in the first place? (True, incidentally.) How many of us as adults transfer some of those feelings to God? Too much Christianity, I fear, stresses the hideous sufferings of Jesus for our sins so that we ought to be very, very grateful. What about Jesus' delight in us? What about that very natural desire to do something special for the beloved, not to earn gratitude, but to make the other person joyful? Curiously enough, those sorts of moralists are always instructing people not to do good deeds for the sake of thanks, but for the love of righteousness alone. Why should God be less generous?

Beyond gratitude, we tend to experience joy as random, chancy; not under our control. For that very reason, it is hard to say we *ought* to feel it.

But perhaps because of its random and chancy appearance, we who know we live in a random and chancy world ought to pay special attention. I increasingly think that joy is something quite different from happiness – which really does not come into the categories of right and wrong. Joy, rather, grows out of trying to square the circle – trying to live with faith and hope and love in a universe that is entirely 'lucky' (or, of course, unlucky, but probably not).

I want to argue that joy is in fact the only ethical imperative in response to God's love as revealed in the whole created universe. Other ethical obligations spring from other ways in which God has revealed the divine. But look at creation, huge and unmanageable, contingent, impermanent, on the move, forever in the process of making itself into something new. Look at us within that creation: tiny in the vastness, but seeing, describing, singing even, a part of the whole. Look, me. Here now, gone tomorrow. A one-off. Wow. Not to rejoice, not to be joyful, not to practise and develop joy at every opportunity, not to ask for it in prayer, seems to be stupid as well as wrong. Free. Adult. Busy. Loved. And all of it comes into existence by the oddest set of circumstances; by the most intricate and basically amusingly improbable pathways. Wow.

It is the very nature of this joy, born out of risk and uncertainty, that it is very difficult to pin any concrete solid meaning on to it, let alone stabilize it long enough to take a hard look at it. Remember Heisenberg's Uncertainty Principle – at the sub-atomic level you cannot tell both where something is and how fast it is going somewhere else. Joy, it seems to me, is a quantum virtue – elusive, fast, and better known by the 'smears' that its events cause than by its visibility.

None the less, I shall end by boldly outlining an exercise programme for the development of joy muscles, or joy fitness. I am not talking about drumming up a particular emotion, but about training oneself to incorporate and act out a truth. The boundary between the lack of authenticity, insincerity, and hypocrisy, and an honest endeavour to act as we believe we ought even when we do not want to, is always a very narrow one – and it is particularly hard with joy to walk along such a boundary with sober balance. (It is so much easier to practise prudence prudently, than to practise joy prudently.)

The 'joy gym'

Warming-up exercises

1 *Find out and think about one new and preposterous thing every day (something for which the only proper response is 'Wow!')* For example, one of the planet Neptune's moons, Triton, revolves the opposite way to anything else in the solar system, including Neptune itself. Or, despite the fact that in the west we don't find toothlessness remotely attractive, it is the toothless smile of the young child that makes night-feeds tolerable; that is to say, what is really a grim evolutionary survival mechanism, is also a source of delight. Or, the male *Hemilepistus reaumuir*, a type of woodlouse which inhabits the very parched North African desert, and which shares child-care with his partner (practically no other male invertebrates do this). Or, God so loved the world that the word became flesh and dwelt among us full of grace and truth. Or, the name for the kangaroo arose from a misunderstanding: one of Cook's crew asked a native Australian the name of the strange bouncing animal that passed by and was answered 'kangaroo'; years later it transpired that this meant 'I don't understand you.' Or... do it for yourself. These are not miracles, they are just extraordinary facts. This exercise will involve you in reading, looking, thinking, and listening, which are all bonus joys.

2 *Pray a lot.* Ask for the gift of joy. Ask again. Two particular aspects of prayer that seem useful to me here

are *adoration* (that is, prayer that is solely directed to the divine – in which one does not think about oneself even to repent) and *silence*. Huge swathes of the universe are silent; align yourself with your origins. In addition, silence, real silence, makes space for new things to happen rather than to be thought.[9] Even if you don't think you believe that prayer works, or even that God exists, silence is joy inducing.

The stretching exercises

1 *Have some adventures.* 'Safety first' may be a good motto for driving a car, but it is fatal to joyful holiness. Too often we use God as a sort of insurance policy or a child's 'security blanket' to keep away our night fears. But the creation, the Bible, and the lives of the saints all teach us that there is no safety. There is no safety, but in risk there is a risky joy. Children in playgrounds and at fun-fairs like to be a little scared. If we can learn to accept that at the centre there is no safety, no guarantee, then we will not have to waste time bowing down to false gods; instead, we will be free to go out and live courageously at the edge of our present humanity.

Originally an adventure meant something that happened to one outside of one's control, by happenstance or fluke. The adventurers of classical stories are courageous, outrageous, laconic, restless, free-spirited. Most of all they want to know what will happen next. What does happen next is usually pretty horrendous, but this never seems to frighten them off. When did you last think of your maths lesson, your newspaper, or your attendance at church as an adventure? But 'anyone who loves their life will lose it, but anyone who is willing to risk it will gain and keep it'. I should warn you that it is most unlikely that you will be rewarded with a well-bred virgin – they have by and large given up the victim job and are off on adventures of their own. More often, you will get the dragon. No one said that adventuring was safe.

2 *Have some fun.* (Of course, adventures can be fun, too.) When I was trying to learn to pray I was constantly warned against 'feelings', especially intensely pleasurable ones.[10] These were called 'sensible consolations', which does not mean 'reasonable comforts' (as you might reasonably think); it means enjoyable sensations. If you sincerely believe that you have a pure soul, which is just passing through, it is probably a good idea not to have too much fun: the soul might be 'seduced' into preferring life to eternity. But I don't believe that. I believe we should get all the sensible consolations we can lay our hands on. I cannot think of a single good relationship (other than with God) that anyone would expect to be improved by a complete lack of pleasure. The feelings of warmth, recognition, challenge, laughter, beauty, and playfulness are fundamental marks of friendship. They don't work against loyalty and the hard slog of loving – on the contrary, they strengthen and succour it. Going back to that toothless baby for a moment: it is the toothless grin, the deep wriggling joy in the child (plus the bizarrely pleasurable physical sensations of breast-feeding), that help a mother not to leave the little monster to scream its head off. The 'sensible consolations' of nursing a baby seem to be, at least to me, a well-designed evolutionary device to secure the continued attentions of a necessary adult, and – at best – a grace and a joy. Why should God be meaner and more devious than a three-month-old human being? Why, in the light of what we know about who we are, should physical and emotional delight be treated as a snare and a delusion?

It seems to me that the more 'sensible consolations' we can find the better. Our emotions and sensations are part of the creation, so they must be part of the brushstrokes of God's artistry. Life is not a nasty but necessary chore to be hurried through as quickly as possible; and it is insulting to God to act as though it were. (I have already said that we should honour the artist.) Life is an extraordinary thing – built by random chances out of ancient explosions, evacuations, mutations, struggles, and deaths, and it is worthy of our serious attention and enjoyment; our love. We would be both foolish and ungrateful not to seek out and wallow in all that we can find. We should indulge in the consolations of art – including Scripture and liturgy. We should embrace the magical and improbable diversity of matter. We should eat more doughnuts. We should learn to enjoy good sex so much that we do not have such difficulty in identifying and resisting bad sex. We should enjoy – vicariously if we prefer – the sensible consolations of others.

Actually, 14-year-olds on skateboards are highly skilful: if unmolested, the chances of them knocking down old ladies are small. Now compare the expression of those skateboarders – intent, eager, alive – with the unhappy faces of most other pedestrians. No one says you have to ride a skateboard, but how do we manage to get so little pleasure from the blatant pleasures of our co-creators and comrades? I fear the answer is that we don't really like pleasure. A very healthy joy exercise is to do the 'maths' of pleasure – balancing realistically my discomfort against your fun; if I can learn to get fun out of your fun, the sums become more complicated and thus more fun.[11]

3 *Think beyond your skin.* This is quite difficult nowadays. Half the information you receive on a daily basis tells you that you are separate from/other than everything else – that your skin marks a boundary that can only be crossed at grave peril to your sanity. That you and you alone must guard that boundary, and that in preserving your boundaries you can best further the goodness of the world by offering to everyone else the separateness that you explore in yourself: and that

preserving your boundaries, your dignity (personal sovereignty), your self-respect, and your integrity is the most valuable thing you can give to the world. This is called 'individual rights'. The problem is that it is sort-of true, but it has to be heroically balanced against the fact that it is not true at all. This ideal sovereign state does not really exist, as I tried to show in the last chapter. It is a defensive structure against our desperate and plaintive need of each other. One of the joy exercises is to stop feeling so pathetic about what is simply a truth.

I do need community. Not because I am a sad person who has failed to self-realize and self-actuate, but because I only exist because of other people. I become me within a community – both immediate and (very) long term. Since joy is related to truth, I will only be able to develop joy if I acknowledge this fact and exercise my self-in-community even as I recognize my self-as-unique. Thinking beyond your skin involves imagining what it would be like to be other; finding out what it would be like to be other;[12] acknowledging that your other creates the possibility of my uniqueness.

The exercise here is to find some friends – lovers, a child – anyone whom you are even a tiny bit dependent on for your happiness. Or even dependent on just for your pleasure. This is the most effective and the least horrendous way of learning that we never walk alone.

I'd like to underline friendship here. Love (sexual, romantic, and contractual) and children have been better incorporated into culture than friendship; but the way in which science suggests we are invited to be co-creators and colleagues with God means that friendship must take on a new dimension. Honour our friends, the artists of wholeness, as I have suggested we should honour all artists: anyway, having friends is fun.

4 *Be more childlike.* This exercise comes, for Christians, from the highest authority.

I am not here talking about having more fun; I am

talking about something rather more high-minded. For most of my theological life there has been a hideous fashion for what is called 'demythologizing'. Biblical fundamentalists want to strip all poetry out of Scripture; and thence all complexity out of morals. Scientific fundamentalists want to strip all that they call 'myth' out of religion; and presumably out of 'life'. They call myths superstition, irrelevant, childish, immature. They never quite ask what is so self-evidently wonderful about the opposite.

I have a friend whose parents would not let her hang up a stocking for Father Christmas because it 'was a lie'. Somewhere, somehow, they had failed to grasp that the imagination is as much, or more, a part of the creation as the 'non-truthfulness' of Father Christmas. Demythologizers absolutely fail to recognize that a little more attention to, say, lucky (and of course deserving) Daniel surviving the night while the lions prowl and roar would do none of us, child or adult, any harm at all.

We urgently need to reclaim the art of telling and hearing stories about the divine. Imagination, creativity, and narrative seems to be the way that God is and moves in the world of matter.

The naivety of childhood is the naivety of ignorance. We need a new naivety, which is not ignorant, but innocent. Ignorance, for all of us, is a regrettable fact of life, but innocence is demanding virtue: open-minded, simple-minded without loss of knowledge or integrity, becoming a little child again without the protection of lack-of-data.

This really requires hours in the 'joy gym': to develop a will, a desire, and a determination to find the world beautiful, magical, wild beyond dreams, dancing its complex patterns of truth; living in the present precisely because one loves the past and desires the future.

To give up power and control.

To offer an enormous toothless grin to the universe in the belief that it will be delighted to oblige.

It feels hideously risky. But there is nothing to be afraid of in a world that is so intricately wrought that 'all things work together' (the 'for good' may require a touch of faith, but the first half of the quotation is just so). If you want to believe in God, there is no reason not to, but do try to believe in a God worthy of the extraordinary universe that we have.

There is indeterminacy, and random mutation, and generosity and chance. There is risk and beauty and joy. Gambling on the God who has so gambled on us may not seem such long odds in the end.

Notes

Introduction

1 For example, *God for the 21st Century*, ed. R. Stannard (SPCK, 2000).
2 Psalm 94.8–11.
3 Although we have got less good even at these recently: what the builders of, for example, Lincoln Cathedral, with its innovative stone-vaulted roof, would have said about our dislike of 'modern' church architecture, and high-tech solutions, is an interesting question.
4 *Myth of Sisyphus* by A. Camus (Gallimard, 1942), trans. Justin O'Brien (Penguin Classics, 2000), p. 25.
5 Many thanks to Jim Turner, Director of the Erasmus Institute at Notre Dame, Indiana, for this perception.
6 Of which, for the developed world, the most precious is too often forgotten: we have reached a point where we can properly expect that any children we have will grow up. I shall come back to this, but we do not often enough celebrate it; it has changed so much sorrow into joy that we can hardly even recognize it as gift.
7 Whichcote. For a fuller discussion of the role and meaning of 'reason' in pre-scientific English, see Basil Willey, *The Seventeenth Century Background* (Chatto & Windus, 1934), especially chapters 7 and 8.
8 Jeremy Taylor, *Ductor Dubitantium*, book II, c. 1, r. 1. The sharp-eyed reader may note that Taylor's 'reason' has quite a lot in common with Einstein's 'observer'.

Theology and Science

1 I shall be coming back to what God is and what a singularity is shortly. Bear with me.

2 Genesis 1.26–7 and Genesis 2.5–24.

3 Kenneth Clark, *Civilization* (John Murray, 1969).

4 ad 185–c. 254.

5 Quoted in P. Davies, *The Mind of God* (Simon & Schuster, 1992), p. 223.

6 You can see this process in some pre-Renaissance Western paintings – which may illustrate, for instance, Mary Magdalene meeting the risen Jesus in the Garden, while somewhere else in the picture the crucifixion is still going on.

7 I have to say I have never been able to see through the geometric patterns, and this annoyed me very much. I even came to believe that it was a modern version of 'The Emperor's New Clothes' – and that we were all being conned whatever my friends told me (a trust issue!). So for me, this description of God's creative work can only be an analogy, not an experience.

8 Stephen Hawking, *A Brief History of Time* (Bantam Books, 1988), p. 140.

9 Ibid., p. 174.

10 Paul Davies, 'What Happened Before the Big Bang?', in *God for the 21st Century*, ed. R. Stannard (SPCK, 2000), p. 10.

11 Ibid., p. 12.

12 Euclid, *c.* 300 BC.

13 There are a number of good examples other than Dava Sobel's *Longitude* (Fourth Estate, 1995) of this peculiar phenomenon. In Mandarin China there were two calendars because the 'perfect' philosophical calendar was so wildly inaccurate that it was disabling agriculture: rather than abandon the idealist calendar, they simply introduced a practical but 'inferior' alternative. Another example, perhaps more relevant to this book, is the fact that Cardinal Bellarmine, who led the attack on Galileo with extraordinary vigour

and enthusiasm, had looked through Galileo's telescope. He had seen the moon of Jupiter orbiting their planet, and had explicitly agreed that they were indeed revolving round it (and therefore not round the earth which was the whole issue). This did not stop him persecuting Galileo – not for saying they revolved, but for saying that the Church (the intellectual elite) was wrong to say they didn't. He militantly preferred the 'authorized version', the intellectual purity, to the physical evidence.

14 John Barrow, *Pi in the Sky* (Oxford University Press, 1993), p. 8.

15 Jain philosophy has always taught something like this. They argue that, when it comes to testing the truth or otherwise of any statement, there are seven recognized positions:
   1 maybe it is true
   2 maybe it is not true;
   3 maybe it is true, but it is not;
   4 maybe it is indeterminate;
   5 maybe it is true but it is indeterminate;
   6 maybe it is not true, but it is indeterminate;
   7 maybe it is true and it is not true and it is indeterminate.

16 D. Hofstadter, *Metamagical Themas* (New York, 1985), p. 485.

17 Quoted in Davies, *The Mind of God*, p. 93.

18 S. L. Maitland, *Home Truths* (Chatto & Windus, 1993).

19 K. Devlin, *Mathematics: The New Golden Age* (Pelican, 1988), p. 49.

20 Davies, in *God for the 21st Century*, p. 48.

21 G. H. Hardy, *A Mathematician's Apology* (Penguin, 1940).

22 CERN (Conseil European pour la Recherche Nucleaire) is the organization that owns the Swiss LEP (Large Electron Positron) accelerator: 'the world's largest scientific machine'. It is a vast circular tunnel 100 metres

underground and 27 kilometres in circumference.

23 It is not at all a coincidence that we now use the word 'astronomical' to mean 'huge', or even 'startlingly huge', but here I do actually mean 'the studying of the stars'.

24 Cf. Michael Poole, 'The Universe as a Home for Life', in *God for the 21st Century*, pp. 15–18.

25 Ibid.

26 Actually there are a number of distinctly odd things about water (bear in mind that water is absolutely essential to life, at least as we live it). In addition to this density curio, it has a very high specific heat (which means that a comparatively large quantity of heat is needed to increase the temperature of water). The amount of heat necessary to change ice to water, and water to steam, is also very high: these thermal features minimize temperature variations – making life on this planet not only possible, but a great deal more agreeable. Cf. Marco de Villiers, *Water* (Houghton Mifflin, 2000), e.g. p. 32.

27 None of this is meant to suggest that I have the slightest doubt of either the integrity or the brilliance of much contemporary quantum physics – *nor of its truth*. I am only trying to say that I am forced into a more difficult position in relation to faith here than I am in relation to faith in the religious experiences of the Doctors of the Church. I have some primitive and incompetent, emotional, and physical experience of religious ecstasy, and I have it within a tradition that has argued that we do not expect to prove the existence of God by any known deductive or inductive reasoning. I have no parallel physical, sensory, or emotional experience of the mystery of the sub-atomic world: I have to take someone else's word for it, even though that word is spoken within a tradition that has consistently argued that there is no such thing as blind faith, and that you can get there by deductive reasoning or by Popper's predictive testing. In our

present culture there is no other field in which I would be expected to believe something just because the person (people) who were telling me were technically more accomplished than I was. To pretend that this is not a problem is unfair and stupid.

28 You have to feel a bit sorry for Rutherford whose remarkable genius was rather overshadowed by Einstein's: it clearly irritated him. A journalist once asked him if he agreed that there were only three people in Britain who were capable of understanding Einstein's general relativity theory. After a pause, he asked: 'Who's the third?'

29 Davies, in *God for the 21st Century*, p. 61.

30 No animals were hurt in the making of this experiment. Schrodinger's cat was not a real cat.

31 It is interesting how often the discoverers of new things cannot cope with the consequences of their ideas: Newton went on being a pre-Newtonian, delving into mystical alchemy, a loving God, and the effectiveness of prayers. Einstein went on being a good Newtonian, insisting that there had to be a cause in order for there to be an effect.

32 Gary Zukav, *The Dancing Wu Li Masters* (William Morrow, 1979), p. 93.

33 Annie Dillard, *Pilgrim at Tinker's Creek* (Picador, 1976), p. 134.

Home on the Range

1 Francis Thompson, *No Strange Land.*

2 This is a rather Western slant on the story: the hellenic philosophical version. It is alien to a traditional Hebrew version, but not fundamentally alien to a Buddhist or Hindu description – even though the understandings of 'God' are radically different in those religions.

3 A very complex version of this second position says that 'we' are insignificant: we are just places for genes to hang out in; genes are busy about a single task,

which is replicating themselves, and they have 'designed' human beings in order to do so most effectively.

4 Some individuals may establish a reputation for telling the story (the Brothers Grimm, for example, or Homer), editing it, shaping it, making it available for a particular audience; their authority rests on *not* claiming that they made it up.

5 It is always a man: I think there are a number of reasons for this, but one of them is that a woman will be drafted in to offer the alternative model of cow-like docility and love: you could not do that very persuasively with a man.

6 The salt wastes where the Aral Sea used to be is a case in point. A little irrigation scheme, to enable a bit more food to be grown – good; a dam here, a reservoir there – and the next thing you know there is no agriculture; no life. The Aral Sea is a high-speed man-made desert. BSE is actually another example: give beef cattle high-level protein in order to fatten them up more quickly, more cheaply – good: no one thought it might be a good idea to test the theory for potential snags before they started shoving sheep offal into the cows.

7 *What Will Happen to God* by William Oddie (DLT, 1986) is a good case in point. Oddie produces here an almost bizarre conspiracy theory in which feminism not only sets out to undermine God, but apparently has great hopes of success. It seems to me that feminism may be right or wrong, and may (probably will) seriously threaten Bill Oddie's personal sense of superiority, but it does seem, at best, improbable that a smallish group of late-twentieth-century women, so divided among themselves that they had not been able to organize a national conference in over ten years, was likely to succeed in eliminating the God who made them.

8 We must not let our suspicions run away with us though. I have lived my adult life in the assumption

that – barring hideous events, against which I might rail to heaven – my babies would grow up. I cannot see this as other than a benefit and one that I owe entirely to the application of scientific knowledge gained in the last century.

9 'The yuck factor' (introduced to me by Matt Hoffman) describes the immediate strong feeling of revulsion that some ideas give us. Sometimes this is well founded (genocide gives many of us a strong 'yuck' factor even when it takes place many miles away or for reasons we know we do not understand). At other times the response turns out to be unfounded, or perhaps well founded, but not precisely applicable to the situation that seems to have provoked it. What such a response calls for is the application of a more analytical examination. The problem is that people who disagree with one's position tend to dismiss the 'yuck' as an 'emotional response' – it is indeed an emotional response but that does not seem a reason to dismiss it; but, rather, a reason to investigate it.

10 The Turing Test was named after Alan Turing, the mathematician and code breaker who developed a theoretical computer and was a strong believer in artificial intelligence. It was he who proposed this humane understanding of intelligence.

11 So far no machine has passed its Turing Test: there is considerable debate among researchers as to whether or when this might happen, but the fact that it has not happened yet should *not* be regarded as proof either that it will or that it won't. In a limited field – that of chess playing – computers have now defeated the world's 'best'.

12 *Laughter: A Scientific Investigation*, by Robert Provine (Faber & Faber, 2000).

13 Annie Dillard, *Pilgrim at Tinker's Creek* (Picador, 1976), pp. 119–24.

14 One hundred and fifty years later Owen's and Lamarck's positions are held by hardly anybody – at

least consciously; quite a lot of people have emotional time for some of Lamarck's ideas, such as 'evolution by desire' (every species desires, of its nature, to improve, get better, climb the ladder in its own specific way): many people cope with ideas of being descended from single-celled organisms by way of gibbons by seeing this as a steady improvement almost of a moral kind, rather than just a random shift or two.

15 On a trip to Switzerland in 1815, Percy Shelley wrote after his name in all the hotel registers 'Democrat, Great Lover of Mankind and Atheist'. He wrote in Greek, but that did not stop a nineteenth-century equivalent of a gossip columnist taking him to task in the English press. (Who says the hounding of media celebrities is a modern scourge?)

16 There are some parallels with Hawking's *A Brief History of Time*. But there are differences – one is that Hawking was making available to the general public what was already in the scientific domain – Darwin was writing for both the popular and the scientific community at the same time.

17 Darwin was famous for his observational skills. You could say that he used the method I have been advocating in this book: he looked at what was there and drew opinions from that, rather than having theories to which chosen data were appended. The merits of the method are proved by Darwin's extraordinary success; although there have been modifications to his theory (particularly the idea that catastrophic events speeded up the process), its basic thesis remains unshaken. This is especially interesting because – on his own admission – he had no idea how or why the necessary mutations happened. It was not until a century later that the discovery of DNA provided an explanation: genes were the something to do the mutating, and they did do it on a regular basis.

18 'Adapted' has no abstract or moral content: Darwin meant suitable, appropriate to the specific environment

in which the species happened to be. He based a great deal of his theory on the differences between sub-species of birds on different Pacific islands: no one species was 'fitter' in the way we tend to use the word now, just better suited, more tightly woven into the place they were in which everything else was evolving too.

19 I once had an argument with a five-year-old niece who got agitated because I did not call my sister 'Mummy'. She isn't my mummy, I argued. But when you are five, people *are* what they are to you. It was not imaginable that her mummy could be something else to someone else. But we are not five and should not behave as we sometimes do: if God is the God of the old red stars, then it is not reasonable to ask them to heat up, grow, accumulate mass and pressure and heat, and explode – just so that I can evolve. A God who destroyed so much for the sole intention of creating early-second-millennium human beings is a stranger God than one who plays dice – since that argument suggests that the creation could have been done far more economically!

20 That's a rhetorical question: a flourish by the author. To be honest, there are, as a matter of fact, some negative answers. Perhaps our creativity flows not truly by pure chance (whatever it may feel like) because we release our subconscious, which knows/controls in a different but none the less effective way. What could it possibly mean to say that God has a subconscious?

21 Rowan Williams, *Resurrection* (DLT, 1982), p. 39.

22 Here's a problem that would have amused a medieval scholastic – if the soul is indivisible (can't be split) and amoebae have a soul, what happens in the moment of division? (The same problem comes up with identical human twins – they are conceived as a single zygote, which splits some days after conception. The Church has not really come with an answer (and it is hard to see how it can). Surely the moral is that 'ensoulment at conception' is a lousy metaphor to 'image' preciousness and unique qualities of each life form; of each human life.)

23 On Radio 4 in 2000, I heard the most fascinating argument between the novelist Jim Crace and the geneticist Richard Dawkins: both are convinced and committed atheists, whose work is related to their (un)religious faith in very profound ways. What they were arguing about was which of them was the 'real' atheist, the 'best and most fundamental atheist'. It made one realize how completely stupid arguments between different denominations of Christianity must sound to outsiders; but it also demonstrated how important interpretation can be to people, even when it is a demonstration of absence: we really do need to invest in our own myths in quite unexplored and unacknowledged ways.

24 Although it is 'traditional' (and commonplace), such dualism is not, strictly speaking, 'orthodox'. Christianity has always struggled (usually unsuccessfully) to articulate the sense that bodies are good, and will be redeemed along with souls as integrated human beings. Most of the debates about who and what Jesus was that excited so much tension in the early Church were won by the anti-dualists; he was not pure spirit; he was not fake body; he was not God, somehow squashed into a temporary framework. And so on.

25 Phobias are probably only one of many exceptions to this sweeping sentence. They are highly responsive to desensitization and usually do not recur once treated.

26 One of the most basic statements of Christian belief is that 'God is without qualities' – a useful word to embrace all those aspects that humans have and spirits do not have: from facial hair to race and gender. (Oddly enough, the conservatives who want to argue that souls are like God in this are very often exactly the same people who insist that God must be *mal*e – or, at the very least, must be defined in male grammars.)

27 Williams, *Resurrection*, p. 36.

28 What this suggests of course is that for most of us we are not just our roles and functions. The mother's

'motherness' has already been prepared – dare I say fertilized – not just by her own and her partner's sexuality, but by the society around her, her own parents, her education, and so on. In addition, her prior self is not wiped out by becoming 'Mother'. This might help us understand that children are not 'owned'; they, like their parents, are more and other than just 'my child'.

29 Persistent Vegetative States – long-term, irreversible comas. This raises some interesting moral questions about living wills and euthanasia. Your death (however much desired by you) might damage me (emotionally, in terms of employment, or in ways I cannot imagine yet) who has the greater rights. See the final chapter for some moral discussion on this – here I am just arguing that this is how it is.

30 Paul Davies and John Gribben, *The Matter Myth* (Viking, 1991), p. 303.

31 In their own field. There is a problem about mutual respect. If scientists want the rest of us to bow down to their expert knowledge, it would help if they were not so contemptuous of other people's expertise (e.g. theologians and saints). However, given the contempt with which their disciplines were treated when the Church had the upper hand, we should not be surprised at their response now. The two 'sides' are co-creating each other.

32 I have to say that the emotions of many 'God is dead' thinkers (not, I hasten to say, their ideas – which are more challenging and stimulating than I am giving them credit for here) do seem rather adolescent.

33 Of course, in the hands of the God who redeems us we are all children – dependent on grace, mercy, and love. We won't lose this if we 'add on' – *gain* – the realization that in the hands of the same God as revealed in the creation we are responsible adults too: co-creators, colleagues, friends.

34 In *Paradise Lost*, Milton has a powerful poetic attempt

at this argument. Science had recently discovered that the earth was tipped 23½ degrees off its vertical axis – he has the angels being so shocked by Adam's and Eve's behaviour that they tipped the world over, and thus created the seasons.

So What?

1 This process is a bit like telling teenagers that Ecstasy will kill them on the spot. It is observably not true and comes with a heavy load of cultural baggage – for example, if the person telling them this is drinking alcohol. You don't have to have a powerfully logical brain to work out that alcohol is at least as deadly as Ecstasy.

2 It sometimes feels as though the 'audience' had no creative function. Once beyond the kindergarten, children are less and less encouraged to be creative, but even less are they encouraged to be audience to other people's art.

3 It is not an error into which Islam seems to fall! But more and more in the West, people speak of their 'spirituality' as something deeply personal, and as something opposed to their social activity, or even intellectual engagement.

4 It is a little hard to know where to start with this bizarre statement of Margaret Thatcher's. Parliamentary democracy is clearly a 'social' formation, as is nationality. But so is 'the family' – it is both socially formed, and formed to constitute a small-sized 'society', a place where two or more individuals get together.

5 This is important. There is a tendency to lump women and children into the same categories at the political level, as though there were no different interests involved; at the same time, all countries that allow abortion do recognize that at the personal level the two interests may be deeply opposed.

6 To be fair, the Labour government of 1997 has done

better in this respect than the previous government.

7 Quite apart from the other issues that this raises, it is interesting to think about what it says to teenage girls whose pregnancy rates we are supposed to be so concerned about: having a baby is so fundamentally necessary to a woman that it is a health issue?

8 In another argument with my aforementioned son I said something about me being a tax-payer; he then pointed out that he was too (via VAT), but had no representation. This he thought was why people used language about 'youth' of a kind so insulting and discriminatory that it would be criminal to use it about women or ethnic minorities.

9 I have been much helped in this by Zen Buddhists – partly because they are about the only religious group in the world who think that in the best prayer absolutely nothing happens: you are working towards nothing. So you cannot see silence as 'useful', only as silent. This leads to a very powerful quality in collective or group silence that I have not experienced elsewhere. I would like to thank the Zen Community at Throstlehole in Cumbria for their generosity in letting me sit with them and begin to learn this.

10 I do actually know people who were trying to tell me this – that one could not judge the effectiveness of one's struggle to convert one's heart by the intensity of feeling, but only by the fruits of grace.

11 It is also worth noticing that shopping centres, when the shops are closed, are extremely well suited to skateboarding. Parks (with grass and benches) are extremely well suited to sitting about on a late afternoon grumbling about skateboarders. Why do we try to send the skateboarders to the park?

12 Bernard Shaw said, 'Do not do unto others as you would have them do unto you – they may have very different tastes.'

Revelat— of God
c̄ Cosmolog. – Arth